Toy fads

Over the years there have been many toy fads. During the 1940s, people enjoyed simple toys like the Slinky and the Magic 8 Ball. In the 1950s, kids got active with the Hula Hoop and the Frisbee. The 1960s saw the introduction of the Etch A Sketch and radio-controlled cars, while the 1970s were dominated by NERF and Star Wars action figures. It seemed like almost every toy had a television series in the 1980s, be it Care Bears, My Little Pony or Transformers. In the 1990s, toys moved with technology—and you got to feed your Tamagotchi and even talk to your Furby.

Weird fads

There have also been some strange fads. In the 1920s, flagpole sitting was a popular spectator 'sport' for stunt performers and publicity seekers. During the Great Depression of the 1930s, dance marathons became a popular distraction as people danced almost non-stop for hundreds of hours. One marathon even lasted for more than 16 weeks!

Source: Blake's Australian History Guide, p.106, Pascal Press

Self-awareness

English – Language

Australian Curriculum Links: *ACELA1502, ACELA1517*

The article on page 4 discusses the history of fads in Australia. Sonia read it and found it very interesting. She showed it to her family and asked them whether they'd taken part in any of those fads when they were kids. Her mum said she had and that 'Rollerblades were the best toys ever', but Sonia's grandfather disagreed. He said that 'Go-karts were much better than Rollerblades, because you had to make them yourself and that taught you useful skills.' Her uncle said, 'Both of those things were stupid. Nothing beats my old Star Wars light sabre. I've still got it!'

PERSONAL & SOCIAL CAPABILITY

Read the article and answer the following questions.

1 What is a fad?

____

____

2 Which of the following can become fads?

a) toys

b) dances

c) clothing

d) all of the above

3 What is the difference between a fact and an opinion? Is the remark 'Go-karts were much better than Rollerblades' a statement of fact or an opinion?

____

____

____

____

TARGETING GENERAL CAPABILITIES YEARS 5-6 © PASCAL PRESS ISBN: 9781925726237

Self-awareness

What could Sonia's mum have said to show that many people shared her view?

a) Rollerblades were the best toys ever.

b) My best friend and I think Rollerblades were the best toys ever.

c) Most people my age think Rollerblades were the best toys ever.

d) I once read a book that said Rollerblades were the best toys ever.

People generally prefer the toys they enjoyed in their own childhood to toys that they never experienced.

True False

It isn't biased to state that other people's opinions are stupid because they're different to yours.

True False

Subjective language reflects the personal opinions of the writer or speaker, while objective language tries to be more factual.

i. Is the article on page 4 subjective or objective? Do you think this is appropriate for the text type, and why?

____

____

ii. Is Sonia's family discussion subjective or objective? Do you think this is appropriate for the situation, and why?

____

____

Your view

Which of the fads mentioned in the article do you think you would enjoy the most? Give reasons for your answer.

____

____

____

Mathematics – Statistics and Probability

Australian Curriculum Links: *ACMSP118, ACMSP119, ACMSP120, ACMSP144*

The article on page 4 looks at some of the fads that obsessed Australians during the twentieth century. But what about more recent fads? Sonia wanted to know whether some of her favourite games were actually fads, so she did some research. After talking to friends and family and looking on the Internet, she identified some of the biggest fads of the 2010s:

- The Ice Bucket Challenge – buckets of ice-cold water were dumped on people's heads to raise money for charity.
- Pokémon GO – mobile phones were used to chase fictional Pokémon characters in the real world.
- Fidget spinners – hand-held spinning toys, promoted as reducing anxiety and aiding concentration.
- Roller shoes – sneakers with removable wheels built into the heels.
- The floss dance – with fists clenched and arms rigid.
- Dabbing – a dance move where you drop your head into a bent arm while the other arm is held out straight.

Have you ever participated in any of these fads? Which ones?

____

____

How about your classmates? One way to understand people's opinions and behaviour patterns is to collect and analyse data.

Fill in your answers for the Modern Fad Survey by ticking the correct boxes below. Then collect all the answers of your classmates. Surveys are often anonymous, so to keep things private, tell them not to write their names on the questionnaires. They can tick as many boxes as apply, except in question (a), where they should only tick one.

TARGETING GENERAL CAPABILITIES YEARS 5-6 © PASCAL PRESS ISBN: 9781925726237

(a) Do you think you get caught up in fads?

☐ never ☐ sometimes ☐ often ☐ always

(b) Have you ever tried the following activities?

☐ Ice Bucket Challenge ☐ Pokémon GO

(c) Have you ever used either of these toys?

☐ roller shoes ☐ fidget spinners

(d) Which of the following dance moves have you performed?

☐ dabbing ☐ flossing

Once you have the data, you need to keep track of it. An easy way is to see how many people selected each category. Sonia surveyed her class and organised the data into two tables using tally marks as below.
Note: There are 30 children in her class.

Survey question (a)

Participation in fads (i.e. the category)	Number of students (i.e. the tally marks)
never	卌
sometimes	卌 卌
often	卌 ||||
always	卌 |

Survey questions (b), (c) and (d)

Modern-day fad (i.e. the categories)	Number of students (i.e. the tally marks)
Ice Bucket Challenge	|
Pokémon GO	||
Roller shoes	卌 卌 ||
Fidget spinners	卌 卌 卌 卌
The floss dance	卌 卌 卌 卌 ||||
Dabbing	卌 卌 卌 卌 卌 卌

Use the tally tables below to organise the data for your own class.

Survey question (a)

Participation in fads (i.e. the category)	Number of students (i.e. the tally marks)
never	
sometimes	
often	
always	

Survey questions (b), (c) and (d)

Modern-day fad (i.e. the categories)	Number of students (i.e. the tally marks)
Ice Bucket Challenge	
Pokémon GO	
Roller shoes	
Fidget spinners	
The floss dance	
Dabbing	

Self-awareness

It's easier to make sense of data if it is displayed in a graph. For instance, look at the one that Sonia created using the results of her class' survey questions (b), (c) and (d):

Answer the following questions using Sonia's graph.

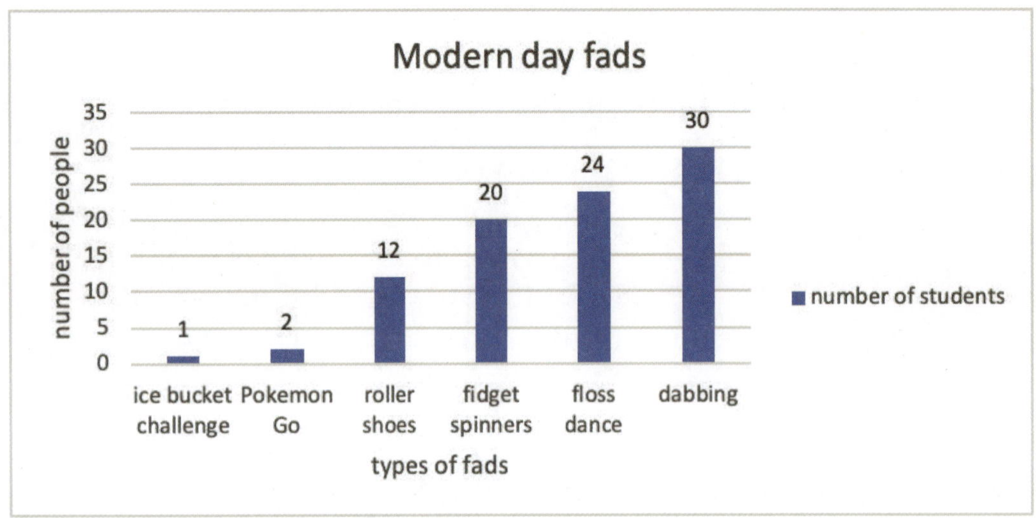

1 What type of graph is this?

a) pie chart

b) scatter graph

c) bar graph

d) line graph

2 What information is given by the vertical axis?

a) the number of times a category was picked

b) the category

3 What information is given by the horizontal axis?

a) the number of times a category was picked

b) the category

4 Which is the most popular fad? i.______________________

Which is the least popular fad? ii.______________________

TARGETING GENERAL CAPABILITIES YEARS 5-6 © PASCAL PRESS ISBN: 9781925726237

Let's assume Sonia's class represents a fair sample of all 11-year-old children in the country.

5 **What is the likelihood or probability that an 11-year-old in Australia has performed the dabbing move? Express your answer as a fraction and as a percentage.**

---

6 **What is the likelihood or probability that an 11-year-old in Australia has used roller shoes? Express your answer as a fraction and as a percentage.**

---

7 **Sonia's question (a) survey shows that five out of the 30 children in her class claim never to have participated in fads. Do you think they were correct? Explain your answer.**

Your class

8 **Create a graph for your class survey results for survey questions (b), (c) and (d). Be sure to fill in all the information: graph and axis titles, numbers and categories.**

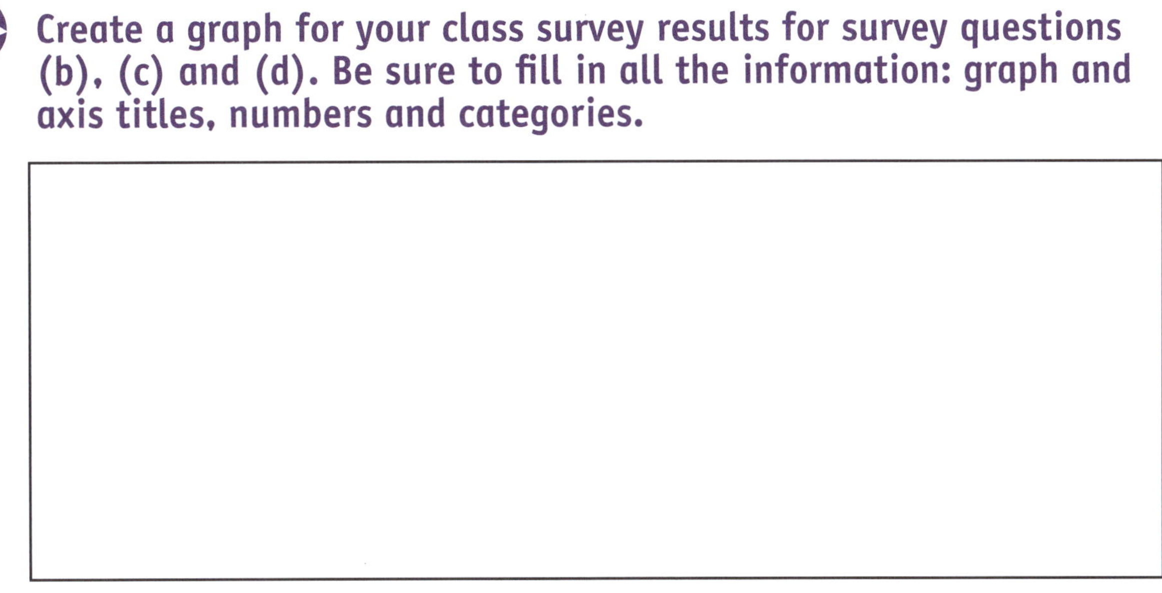

HASS – Economics and Business

Australian Curriculum Links: *ACHASSK119, ACHASSK121, ACHASSK149, ACHASSK150*

Lots of times we hear people say they need something—like a new pair of shoes to wear at a party—but do they really need it, or do they just want it? In Economics, a need is something that is necessary for survival or to meet basic standards of living, while a want is something that's desired but not essential. Often people want to buy things because they're encouraged to do so by social trends, peer pressure and/or advertising. This is especially the case for fads.

It's important to keep in mind that wants are unlimited—we'll never stop wanting things—but resources are limited. If you buy something with your pocket money, such as a fidget spinner, you might not have enough money left to buy something else that you want, such as a snack. This is known as a trade-off. The opportunity cost of buying the fidget spinner is the loss of the item that you've foregone, in this case, a snack.

Explain the difference between a need and a want.

____

____

Are fad toys and fashion items needs or wants? Explain your answer.

____

____

Look at the items listed in the word bank. Are they needs or wants? Put them in the correct place in the table on the next page.

Word bank

water chocolate bar everyday clothes roller shoes staple foods

shoes computer game party dress housing soft drink

TARGETING GENERAL CAPABILITIES YEARS 5-6 © PASCAL PRESS ISBN: 9781925726237

Needs	Wants

Your decision to buy something can be influenced by ...

a) advertising.

b) social trends and peer pressure.

c) how much money you have available.

d) all of the above.

When you want to buy something, it's wise to find out more about the product and compare prices.

True False

Keeping track of how much you spend is a good way to avoid spending too much money on things you don't need.

True False

Why do consumers need to make trade-offs when buying things?

____

____

Your view

Your favourite aunty has just given you $50 to spend on anything you like. Make a list of things you want to buy with your gift. Do you have enough money for everything? Write down what you want the most, and what you are prepared to forego.

____

____

PERSONAL & SOCIAL CAPABILITY

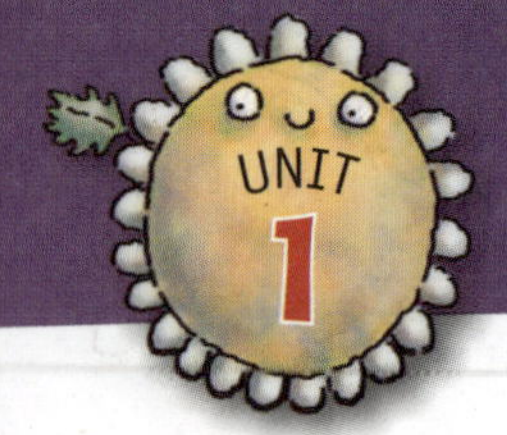

Health & Physical Education

Australian Curriculum Links: *ACPPS054, ACCPPS057*

The 21st century has seen many fads. While most were harmless fun, some were dangerous. People have been hurt and even killed while participating in fads. One of the most dangerous was planking, or lying face down, often in unusual locations. Photographs were shared on social media and planking went viral. It featured in some television shows, and popular musicians also made reference to it, further spreading the craze. Some people planked relatively safely on the floor or on a bed or sofa—but others picked places that were clearly dangerous, such as on railings, clotheslines and even balconies. Tragically, a young man in Brisbane plunged to his death while trying to plank on a balcony railing in an apartment block.

Source: https://www.flickr.com/photos/theeerin/4112368718/in/photostream/ / CC BY-SA (https://creativecommons.org/licenses/by-sa/2.0)

1 Why is planking potentially dangerous?

___

___

___

___

TARGETING GENERAL CAPABILITIES YEARS 5-6 © PASCAL PRESS ISBN: 9781925726237

The ice bucket challenge was a fad that involved emptying containers of ice-cold water over people's heads. What risks are created by this activity?

___

The cinnamon challenge dared people to swallow a teaspoon full of cinnamon powder without water. Can you work out why this is dangerous?

___

Fads are just harmless fun, there's no need to question them.

True False

Just because a celebrity takes part in a fad, it doesn't mean others will copy.

True False

When a fad is shared on social media, people are more likely to try to copy.

True False

If someone encourages you to take part in a new fad, you should ...

a) assess the risks for yourself.

b) seek advice from a responsible adult.

c) refuse to take part if you think it's unsafe.

d) all of the above.

Your view

Can you think of any other fads, recent or not, that were dangerous? List them below.

___

Self-reflection

This unit was about self-awareness. What have you learnt about fads and how you respond to them?

___

___

TARGETING GENERAL CAPABILITIES YEARS 5-6 © PASCAL PRESS ISBN: 9781925726237

Self-management

Harvest time was approaching, and Faruq was looking forward to a bumper crop from his school's kitchen garden. Faruq was one of the keenest members of the gardening team, having put in many hours of dedicated work. He always arrived at school early so that he'd have time to see how the garden was progressing.

To his horror, one morning he found a flock of birds feasting on the peas. Faruq jumped and shouted and managed to shoo them away, but he knew they'd be back later when the school was empty. That evening, Faruq surfed the Internet looking for ideas that could help him protect the garden. He came across the following blog post and decided to give it a go.

HOW TO MAKE A SCARECROW

What you need:

- old pillowcase
- old long-sleeved shirt
- old pair of trousers
- old socks and gloves
- straw or pillow stuffing
- string or gardening twine
- sewing needle and thread
- buttons for eyes
- permanent marker
- long garden stake
- old hat

What to do:

1. Fill the pillowcase with straw and tie it firmly with string.
2. Fill the shirt, do up the shirt buttons, tie a string around each cuff, tie a string around the waist to hold in the stuffing.
3. Fill the trousers and tie up the cuffs.
4. Push the shirt into the trousers' waistband and sew the pieces together.
5. Sew old socks over the trouser cuffs.
6. Sew gloves over the sleeve cuffs.
7. Sew buttons onto the pillow as eyes.
8. Draw on the remaining facial features with a marker.
9. Push the head into the shirt's collar and stitch in place.
10. Press the garden stake firmly in its desired location.
11. Tie the scarecrow to the garden stake.
12. Place the hat on its head and let it do its stuff!

TARGETING GENERAL CAPABILITIES YEARS 5-6 © PASCAL PRESS ISBN: 9781925726237

English – Language

Australian Curriculum Links: *ACELA1504, ACELA1524*

Faruq got permission to make a scarecrow to guard the school's kitchen garden. He tried following the blog post's instructions but discovered that, once he got down to it, they weren't at all easy to follow. Stuffing kept poking out and pieces kept coming apart. It felt like a huge waste of time and effort. There were moments when Faruq felt like giving up, but then he remembered how hard he'd worked and how much he wanted to succeed. After a few frustrating days of trial and error, he finally succeeded in making a sturdy scarecrow. The school's peas were safe!

Read the blog post on page 16 and answer the following questions.

1 What type of text is this?

a) informative

b) persuasive

c) imaginative

d) all of the above

2 The text can best be described as a …

a) recount.

b) procedure.

c) narrative.

d) discussion.

3 How is the text structured?

a) paragraphs

b) verses and a chorus

c) dialogue

d) steps to follow

Self-management

4. What is the purpose of the text?

____

____

5. Do you think the blog post's written instructions are easy to follow without the help of illustrations? Why or why not?

____

____

____

____

____

6. Number the following illustrations, placing them in the correct order (a) to (e).

☐ 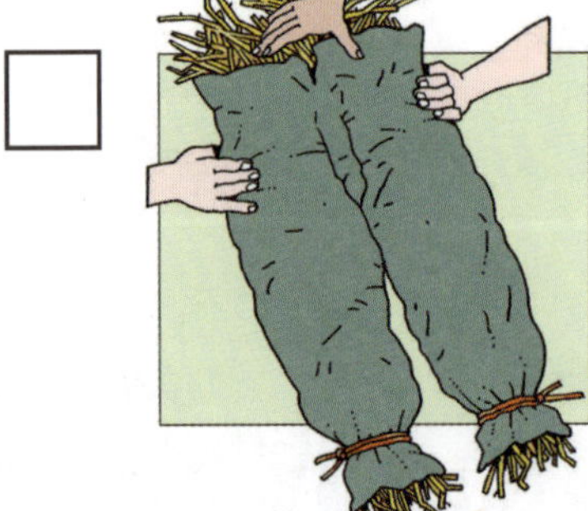

☐ 

☐ 

☐

☐

TARGETING GENERAL CAPABILITIES YEARS 5-6 © PASCAL PRESS ISBN: 9781925726237

Some concepts are easier to express with images than by written words alone.

True False

Your turn

8 **Without the help of diagrams, write a set of numbered instructions that explain how to tie up a pair of shoelaces.**

Do you think that you could follow the instructions if you'd never seen anybody tie up shoelaces before? Why or why not?

HASS – Geography

Australian Curriculum Links: *ACHASSK112, ACHASSK113, ACHASSI127, ACHASSI132*

Humans organise spaces by creating zones. Similar activities are grouped together in the same zone. For example, people live in residential zones and they shop in commercial zones. People who plan these zones are called urban planners or town planners. When deciding where to put each zone, planners take into account the landscape features of the area and the needs of the people who will live there.

Zone	What is found in the zone?	Notes
Residential	Homes: houses, apartments, townhouses, high-rise apartment blocks, etc.	There are often restrictions on the height, type and style of buildings in these zones.
Commercial	Businesses: shopping centres, petrol stations, offices, etc.	These zones often include a main street and are located near residential zones as people don't like to travel to shop and work.
Industrial	Manufacturing and warehouses: transport depots, factories, warehouses, storage facilities, airports, etc.	These zones can be dangerous, noisy and smelly, so they are usually located a long way from residential zones.
Green	Open land or parks: sports fields, gardens, nature reserves, etc.	These zones are often found near residential areas. Green spaces in the city are often small as land is expensive.
Special purpose	Community services: hospitals, post offices, police stations, fire stations, churches, schools, etc.	These zones are often near residential areas as they provide services for the community.

Source: Australian Geography Centres, Upper Primary, p.21, Blake Education

TARGETING GENERAL CAPABILITIES YEARS 5-6 © PASCAL PRESS ISBN: 9781925726237

What type of zoning does a school have?

a) residential

b) commercial

c) special purpose

d) industrial

2 **Why are schools often found near residential areas?**

____

____

3 **What two things are considered when planning a town?**

i. ______________________________________

ii. ______________________________________

Faruq's school is located in a busy inner-city area. Describe the likely environment of such an area.

____

____

Faruq lives in a small apartment near his school. Why do you think he is so keen on the school's kitchen garden?

____

____

It doesn't matter where you live, you can find access to activities that you enjoy.

True False

What features are required for a school kitchen garden to thrive?

a) adequate sun

b) access to water

c) access to classrooms

d) all of the above

PERSONAL & SOCIAL CAPABILITY

Your view

8 Sketch a map of your school and label the main buildings and grounds. Where would be a good place to add a kitchen garden? Show it on the map and give reasons for your decision.

PERSONAL & SOCIAL CAPABILITY

Science

Australian Curriculum Links: *ACSSU043, ACSSU094*

Faruq's class carried out a science experiment to help them work out what plants need to survive and thrive. They took four pots filled with fertilised potting mix and planted identical tomato seedlings into each pot.

One pot was the control for the experiment: it would be given everything a plant needs to survive, i.e. water, air, sunlight and food. The other pots would each have a different one of these factors removed (except for food, which they all had in the potting mix).

They labelled the pots 1 through to 4, and took the following action:

- Pot 1 – watered and placed in a sunny position outside
- Pot 2 – placed next to pot 1, but not watered
- Pot 3 – watered and placed next to pot 1, but the pot was placed inside a large plastic bag which was then tightly sealed
- Pot 4 – watered and placed in a dark cupboard.

Each pot was watered at the same times except for pot 2, which was never watered. The class kept records of their observations for eight weeks, then they selected the healthiest surviving plants and placed them in the school's kitchen garden.

Why does it matter that the plants in each pot were identical at the start of the experiment?

____

____

Which pot was the control?

a) pot 1 b) pot 2 c) pot 3 d) pot 4

Which factor was removed from pot 3?

a) water b) air c) sunlight d) food

Self-management

 Which factor was removed from pot 4?

a) water b) air c) sunlight d) food

 Which plant do you think grew the best? Why?

____

____

 Which plant/s do you think grew nearly as well as the best plant, and which do you think might not have survived at all? Explain your answer.

____

____

 What sort of commitment is required to plant and maintain a vegetable garden?

____

____

Your turn

 Perform the experiment yourself, following the steps outlined above. Once a week, take observations of the conditions of your plants and record them in the table below.

	Pot 1	Pot 2	Pot 3	Pot 4
Week 1				
Week 2				
Week 3				
Week 4				
Week 5				
Week 6				
Week 7				
Week 8				

What did you learn from this about the care you need to take to ensure plants grow and thrive?

____

____

TARGETING GENERAL CAPABILITIES YEARS 5-6 © PASCAL PRESS ISBN: 9781925726237

Technologies – Design and Technologies

Australian Curriculum Link: *ACTDEK019*

PERSONAL & SOCIAL CAPABILITY

Growing your own fruit and vegetables contributes to a sustainable future by reducing the need for long-distance shipping and storage of food—but that in itself isn't enough to ensure sustainability. It's important that a kitchen garden is designed with that specific aim in mind. This involves choosing plants that suit the area's climatic and soil conditions, as well as making smart decisions when the garden is first set up.

Australia is a dry continent, so watering solutions are essentials. Possible solutions include the use of rainwater tanks, grey water and tailored irrigation systems. Mulching also helps save water by reducing the amount of water that evaporates from the soil. Compost works in a similar way, and it also provides nutrients to the plants and improves the soil. Compost can be made in homes or at schools out of kitchen scraps, garden waste and leftover cardboard.

How does locally grown produce improve sustainability?

____

____

What are two factors that should be considered when selecting plants for a kitchen garden?

____

____

The climatic conditions of a region include patterns in ...

a) temperature.

b) precipitation.

c) humidity.

d) all of the above.

Which of the following is NOT a kitchen garden watering solution?

a) rainwater tanks

b) grey water

c) water heating

d) irrigation systems

Mulching increases the amount of water that soil loses due to evaporation.

True False

'Grey water' is wastewater that comes from baths, dishwashers, sinks and washing machines. It does not include water from toilets. Why do you think it isn't a good idea to use toilet wastewater in gardens?

Write a list of goals that you would set if you were designing a kitchen garden for your school.

Your turn

Research how to create compost. Write a plan for how you could create compost in your home garden or at your school in the space below. Be sure to consider:

- **the space you have available**
- **the materials you have available**
- **any safety issues that may arise.**

Health & Physical Education

Australian Curriculum Links: *ACPPS058, ACPPS059*

The Australian Dietary Guidelines provide information about foods that protect your health and improve your wellbeing. Eating well can reduce the risk of diet-related conditions, such as high blood pressure and cholesterol, and reduce the risk of chronic diseases, such as type 2 diabetes, cardiovascular disease and some cancers. It's also important to be physically active and to create connections with others to enhance social health.

Source: https://www.dropbox.com/sh/hrkzhyla7qoct3q/AABMc8SRKmtVf0w5MmfpQQcYa?dl=0

Under the Australian Dietary Guidelines, which food groups should we be eating the most of? What are some examples?

___

___

The guidelines also recommended that we drink plenty of ...

a) milk. b) soft drink. c) water. d) olive oil.

Identify some of the foods that we should only eat sometimes and in small amounts.

___

___

Self-management

4 Which of the above food groups could you grow in a kitchen garden?

___

5 Apart from healthy food, name two other benefits that can be obtained through a school or community kitchen garden.

i. ___

ii. ___

6 Participating in outdoor activities such as gardening can be detrimental to your health and wellbeing.

True False

7 Being fit and healthy makes it easier for you to achieve your goals in life, as it can make you stronger and more resilient.

True False

Your turn

8 You've been asked to talk at assembly about the need for a school kitchen garden. Write a speech to encourage other students to join in and support your goal.

___

___

___

___

Self-reflection

This unit was about self-management. What have you learnt about your ability to achieve your goals, even when things get difficult?

___

___

___

___

TARGETING GENERAL CAPABILITIES YEARS 5-6 © PASCAL PRESS ISBN: 9781925726237

YOUNG PEOPLE LEAD THE WAY FOR CLIMATE CHANGE

Hundreds of thousands of young people around the country have taken to the streets to demand immediate action in the latest wave of climate strikes, bringing the CBDs of Sydney, Melbourne and Brisbane to a grinding halt.

Inspired by Swedish teenage activist, Greta Thunberg, Australian students have walked out of school and university classes to have their voices heard.

'I don't care if I get expelled,' says 16-year-old Dylan Miller, who joined the protests. 'There's no future for me anyway because climate change is destroying the planet.'

Ming Chan, 17, also had something to say. 'I'm too young to vote, but by joining the marches I can show how I feel about the government's failure to secure our future.'

The protestors are calling on the Australian government to commit to a fossil-free future, with no new oil, coal and gas projects to be implemented. 'We demand 100 per cent renewable energy generation by the year 2030,' Chan explains.

Millions of people throughout the world have shown support for the cause through social media or by joining marches, but not everybody agrees with the climate strikers.

'If they want to save the world, they should go to uni and learn how to make renewable energy viable,' says accountant John Kowalski. 'Sure, climate change is a problem, but dropping out of classes and throwing tantrums isn't going to help anybody.'

'I care about the environment, but I'm worried about the effect of the strikes on children,' says mother of two, Camilla Smythe. 'All this climate anxiety isn't good for them; it's making them lose hope.'

'It's outrageous,' says Robin Voyle, spokesperson for the Climate Sceptics Thinktank. 'Everyone knows climate change isn't real. This is just a stunt, led by troublemakers.'

Stunt or not, with emotions running as high as global temperatures, there's no sign that the climate strikes will stop anytime soon.

English – Literature

Australian Curriculum Links: *ACELT1609, ACELT1611, ACELT1795, ACELY1711, ACELY1801*

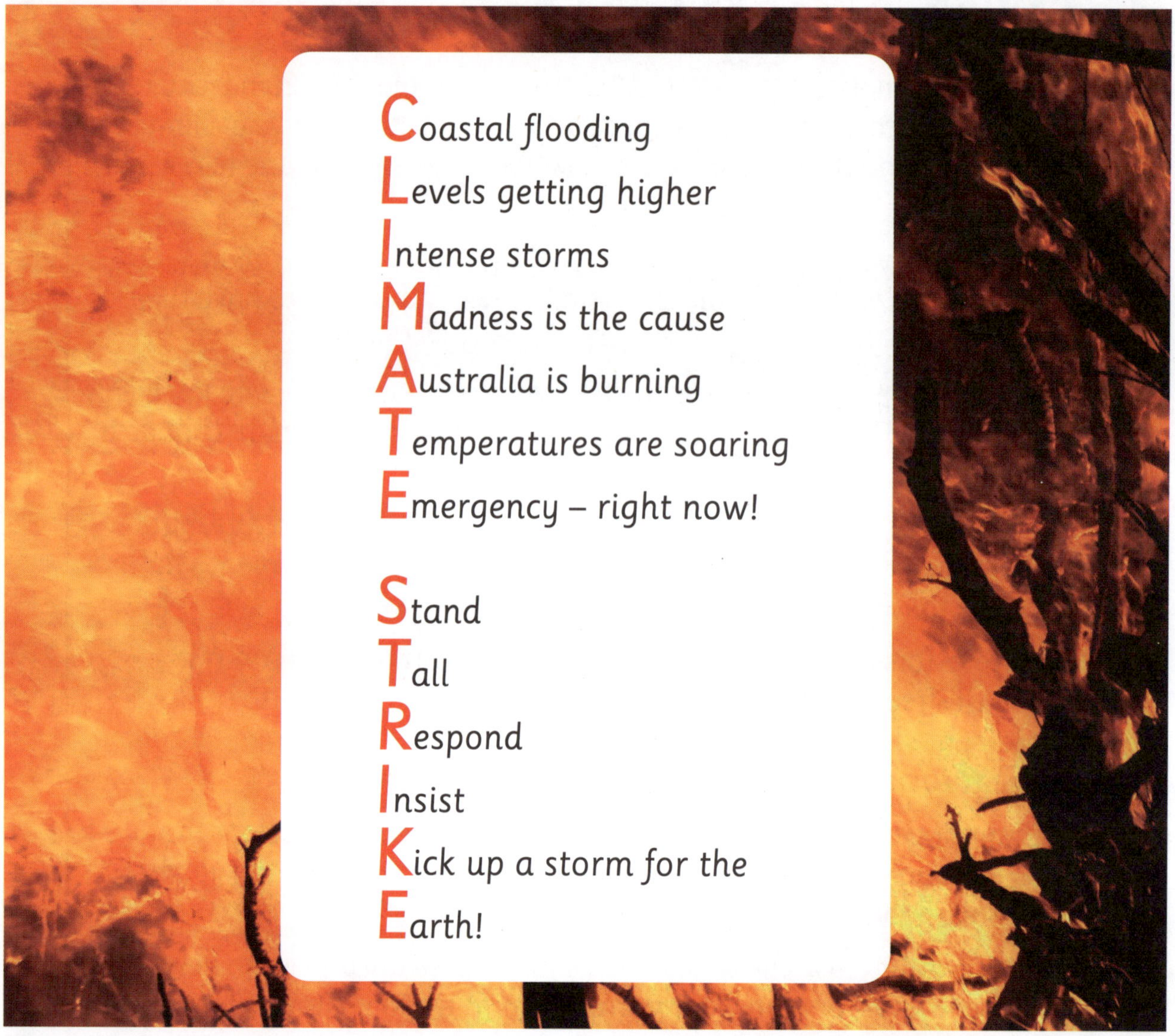

Coastal flooding
Levels getting higher
Intense storms
Madness is the cause
Australia is burning
Temperatures are soaring
Emergency – right now!

Stand
Tall
Respond
Insist
Kick up a storm for the
Earth!

Read the poem above and answer the following questions.

What type of poem is this?

a) rhyming
b) free form
c) acrostic
d) haiku

TARGETING GENERAL CAPABILITIES YEARS 5-6 © PASCAL PRESS ISBN: 9781925726237

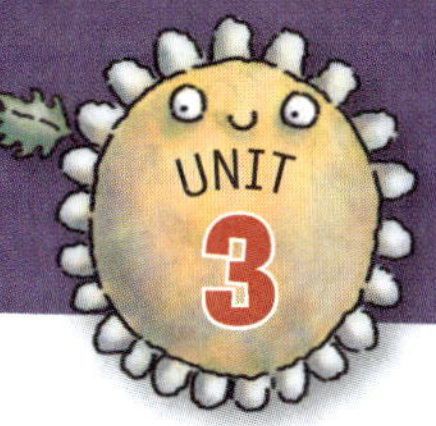

2 Who may have written the poem?

a) a climate change protestor

b) a climate change sceptic

c) a petroleum engineer

d) someone with no opinion on climate change

3 What is the purpose of the poem?

____

4 The poem is in two stanzas. Which stanza …

i. identifies some of the impacts of climate change? ______________

ii. is a call for action? ______________

5 List examples of emotive words and phrases used by the poet to express their point of view.

____

____

6 The line 'Australia is burning' is meant to …

a) show temperatures are rising across the country.

b) refer to the bushfires and link them to global warming.

c) literally mean the country is on fire.

d) both a and b.

7 The second stanza is mostly composed of single-word lines, increasing the pace of the poem. Why do you think the poet did that?

____

____

Your view

8 Do you agree or disagree with the poet's point of view? Explain your answer.

____

____

HASS – Civics and Citizenship

Australian Curriculum Links: *ACHASSK115, ACHASSK118, ACHASSK147, ACHASSK148*

Australia is a representative democracy—meaning that everyone aged 18 and over gets to vote for who they want to represent them in parliament. Our system is underpinned by basic democratic rights, including freedom of speech and freedom of assembly. In other words, people have the right to gather in a public place for the purpose of a peaceful protest. They are allowed to express their dissatisfaction and speak out against laws and government policies that they disagree with. Climate strikes are legal, and some people insist they are needed to save the planet. However, as the news article on page 29 shows, not everyone agrees with the protests, and their reasons for disagreeing vary.

Read the article on page 29 and answer the following questions.

What was the purpose of the climate strikes?

____

____

Climate strikes are illegal, and protestors can be fined for taking part.

True False

Freedom of speech and freedom of assembly are essential features of Australian democracy.

True False

How can people with shared beliefs and values work together to achieve their civic goals?

a) join peaceful demonstrations

b) sign petitions

c) share campaigns through social media

d) all of the above

TARGETING GENERAL CAPABILITIES YEARS 5-6 © PASCAL PRESS ISBN: 9781925726237

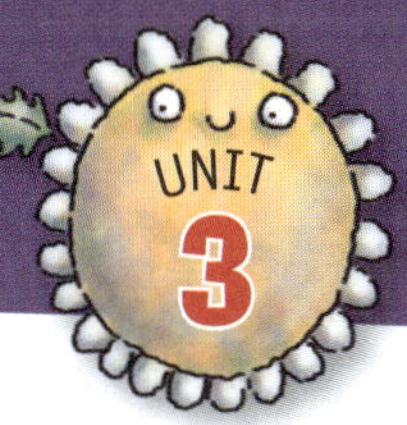

5 **Ming Chan was too young to vote, so what method did she choose to express her views about climate change?**

a) She wrote a letter to the prime minister.

b) She joined the climate strike march.

c) She wrote a news article.

d) She started a riot.

6 **Three people who disagreed with the climate strike were quoted in the article. What reasons did they give for disagreeing?**

i. ______________________________

____

ii. ______________________________

____

iii. ______________________________

____

Were the reasons basically the same or different?

____

7 **Is climate change a national or global issue, or a combination of both? Explain your answer.**

____

____

Your view

8 **What are your views on the climate strikes? Do you think they're a good way to address the issue of climate change? Why or why not?**

____

____

____

____

Science

Australian Curriculum Links: *ACSSU078, ACSSU096*

The Earth is one of eight planets that orbits our star, the sun. As far as we know, it's the only place in the solar system that's the right temperature to sustain life. This is partly because we orbit at the right distance from the sun, and partly because our atmosphere acts like a greenhouse. Gases such as carbon dioxide and methane, known as greenhouse gases, absorb heat energy from the sun and re-radiate it, keeping the Earth's surface warm. They occur naturally, but they're also created by human activity.

As long as greenhouse gas levels stay steady, the Earth's climate remains fairly stable. But since the Industrial Revolution, the amount of carbon dioxide in the atmosphere has increased sharply—this is called the enhanced greenhouse effect. The planet has experienced a rise in the average global temperature by about one degree centigrade since the late 1800s. This may not seem like much, but climate scientists have linked this to rising sea levels, more frequent and severe extreme weather events and longer, harsher droughts and bushfires.

Which body provides heat energy in our solar system?

a) the Earth

b) the sun

c) the atmosphere

d) the sea

2 What are two key reasons why the Earth is at the right temperature to sustain life?

i. ______________________________

____

ii. ______________________________

____

3 **What do you think might happen if the Earth had no greenhouse gases at all? Why do you think this?**

___

___

4 **Greenhouse gases, including carbon dioxide and methane, are only created by human activity; they do not occur naturally.**

True False

5 **Fossil fuels started to be mined and burned in vast quantities during the Industrial Revolution, releasing carbon dioxide into the air.**

True False

6 **Climate scientists have linked an increase in greenhouse gases to ...**

a) rising sea levels.

b) increased extreme weather events.

c) worsening droughts and bushfires.

d) all of the above.

7 **Most scientists believe that the enhanced greenhouse effect is caused by human activity and is causing dangerous climate change.**

i. Do you agree with this view?

___

___

ii. Why do you think some people disagree?

___

___

Your view

8 **Australia is prone to droughts and bushfires, and climate change is expected to worsen both. Have you experienced either in your local community? Describe the steps that you and your family had to take to either save water during a drought or to protect yourselves from a bushfire threat.**

___

___

___

___

Mathematics – Statistics and Probability

Australian Curriculum Links: *ACMSP116, ACMSP114*

Meteorologists consider many factors when they make weather forecasts. Some of the things they look at include current weather patterns, geographical conditions, the type and extent of cloud cover, and areas of high and low air pressure. They look at how strong winds are and in which directions they're blowing over the sea and over the land. Scientific models are then used to predict what the weather outlook will be.

However, weather systems are very complex, and few forecasts can be made with absolute certainty. Instead, meteorologists talk about probabilities— or the chance that a particular weather event will happen. For instance, the forecast for tomorrow might state that there's a 50 per cent chance of rain. Percentages range from 0 to 100 per cent, and the higher the percentage, the more likely it is that the event will happen.

Probabilities can be expressed in the following ways:

- certain – the event will definitely happen
- likely – the event isn't definite, but it's more likely to occur than not
- equally likely – the event is as likely to happen as it is to not happen
- unlikely – the event is more likely to not happen than it is to happen
- impossible – the event will definitely not happen.

A 0 per cent chance of rain means that ...

a) rain is certain.
b) rain is impossible.
c) it's more likely to rain than not rain.
d) it's equally as likely to rain as it is to not rain.

A 100 per cent chance of rain means that ...

a) rain is certain.
b) rain is impossible.
c) it's more likely to rain than not rain.
d) it's equally as likely to rain as it is to not rain.

TARGETING GENERAL CAPABILITIES YEARS 5-6 © PASCAL PRESS ISBN: 9781925726237

A 50 per cent chance of rain means that ...

a) rain is certain.
b) rain is impossible.
c) it's more likely to rain than not rain.
d) it's equally as likely to rain as it is to not rain.

It's easier to understand probability when you look at simple systems—like games of chance. Assume you have a spinner with four colours on it: black, white, red and blue. Whenever you spin it, it lands on one and only one colour. The chance that it will land on red if you spin it once is 1 out of 4 (because it is one out of the four possible outcomes).

Probabilities can be expressed as fractions, decimals or percentages.

Express 1 out of 4 as a fraction. ______________________

To find the decimal, divide the numerator (the number above the line in a fraction) by the denominator (the number below the line). Express 1 out of 4 as a decimal.

____

To find the percentage, you simply multiply the decimal by 100. Express 1 out of 4 as a percentage.

____

Which statement is true, assuming you only spin the spinner once?

a) It is certain that the spinner will land on red that time.
b) It is impossible that the spinner will land on red that time.
c) It is likely that the spinner will land on red that time.
d) It is unlikely that the spinner will land on red that time.

Which is likely to be more accurate: a forecast of tomorrow's weather, or the weather in a week's time? Why do you think this?

____

____

____

Health & Physical Education

Australian Curriculum Links: *ACPPS055, ACPPS056*

Positive relationships are formed when people respect other's opinions. They don't have to always agree on everything, but it helps if they respect each other's rights to express themselves. If they're not allowed to speak out, they may feel unvalued and powerless.

Societies often face challenges or hardships, such as the threats associated with climate change. Strong emotions can arise, born of anxiety and fear of what the future may bring. This makes different people behave in different ways. Some will have a positive response. They'll try to improve things and make a real change. Others might have a negative response, for instance they might become fearful or aggressive. Being aware of why people react the way they do—rather than just focusing on their behaviour—can help members of the community to understand each other.

Read the news article on page 29 and answer the following questions.

1 Dylan Miller didn't care whether he was expelled from school or not because he believed he had no future. Was this a positive or a negative response to the issue of climate change?

____

2 Ming Chan was too young to vote, so she joined the marches to have the opportunity to express her views. Was this a positive or negative response?

____

3 Dylan was probably feeling ...

a) anxious.

b) angry.

c) hopeful.

d) both a and b.

TARGETING GENERAL CAPABILITIES YEARS 5-6 © PASCAL PRESS ISBN: 9781925726237

4 It's possible to predict how a person will feel in any given situation.

True False

5 Strong emotions can influence a person's ability to make wise decisions.

True False

6 John Kowalski was opposed to the marches. He suggested that young people go to university to learn how to make renewable energy viable. Was his remark helpful or unhelpful? Why?

7 Robin Voyle was also opposed to the strikes, calling them a stunt. He insisted that climate change was not real. Was his remark helpful or unhelpful? Why?

Your view

8 A famous philosopher once said, 'I disapprove of what you say, but I will defend to the death your right to say it'. Do you agree or disagree with this view? Explain your answer.

Self-reflection

This unit was about social awareness. What have you learnt about people respecting each other's opinions?

Based on the latest advice from the Chief Health Officer, we've now passed new laws making face coverings mandatory in the metropolitan area. This is due to the alarming spike in COVID-19 cases in recent days, despite going back into lockdown. We've reached record levels of new infections, hospitalisations and deaths, passing grim milestones each day.

Nobody likes going back into lockdown, and it is not a decision we've made lightly. As a reminder, you can currently only leave your home for one of four reasons:

- going to work or study if you can't do it from home
- shopping for essential supplies, such as food or medicine
- exercising in your neighbourhood
- attending medical appointments or providing care.

Otherwise, don't go out. I'll say it again. Don't go out. We're in the middle of a global pandemic. We must take it seriously, or more lives will be lost. Don't go out.

The new face covering laws will apply from midnight Sunday. This gives you plenty of time to go and buy masks, but if you already have one, please start wearing it. From next week, anybody out in the metropolitan area without a mask will be fined $200. Some exemptions will apply—for instance for children aged under 12, for people who are exercising, and for people with certain medical conditions. Otherwise, wear a mask.

You'll be aware by now that businesses in our state have also returned to higher restriction levels. Cafes and restaurants can no longer seat customers; they can only provide takeaway and delivery services. Beauty salons have closed. Entertainment and cultural venues have closed. There is no more community sport. We don't want this to continue any longer than it has to.

We know that times are tough for businesses and workers alike, but we're looking at further avenues of financial support to help you get through. Remember, we're all in this together.

TARGETING GENERAL CAPABILITIES YEARS 5-6 © PASCAL PRESS ISBN: 9781925726237

English – Language

Australian Curriculum Links: *ACELA1501, ACELA1504, ACELA1517, ACELA1518*

To communicate well, it's important to use the right words. People use language differently depending on who it is they are talking to. They might speak formally, using proper words and grammar, or casually, using slang words and informal sentences. The words they choose will depend on how they want people to respond.

It's also important for a writer to understand when it's appropriate to use objective language and when it's acceptable to use subjective language. Objective language states the facts in a straightforward and unemotional manner, while subjective language shows the writer's emotions, opinions and point of view. Objective language tends to be used in factual accounts and news reports so that people are left to make up their own minds about the issue being discussed. Subjective language is more common in opinion pieces and commentaries.

Read the Premier's speech on page 40 and answer the following questions.

Why did the Premier issue this media release?

a) to provide information

b) to persuade people to follow instructions

c) to entertain the public

d) both a and b

The Premier wants people to ...

a) not worry about COVID-19 and live life as usual.

b) spend more money to stimulate the economy.

c) follow the new laws regarding face coverings.

d) open up new businesses.

This media release was most likely written ...

a) when the COVID-19 outbreak was first noticed overseas.

b) when the COVID-19 pandemic first reached Australia.

c) when a second wave of the pandemic hit a particular state.

d) after the pandemic was over.

Is the language used relatively formal or informal? Use examples from the text to support your answer.

____

____

In one paragraph, the Premier says 'don't go out' three times. Which language technique is this?

a) onomatopoeia b) repetition c) alliteration d) simile

Explain the difference between objective and subjective language.

____

____

Are the following phrases from the text objective or subjective?

i. 'we've now passed new laws making face coverings mandatory'

____

ii. 'passing grim milestones each day'

____

Your view

The media release contains both objective and subjective language. Do you think it's appropriate for the Premier to use subjective language in this text? Why do you think that?

____

____

TARGETING GENERAL CAPABILITIES YEARS 5-6 © PASCAL PRESS ISBN: 9781925726237

HASS – History

Australian Curriculum Links: *ACHASSI094, ACHASSI104, ACHASSK135, ACHASSK136*

In 1918, as World War I was drawing to a close, the Spanish flu swept through Europe and then around the world as returning servicemen carried it back to their homes. It's been estimated that around 500 million people—one third of the world's population at the time—were infected. About 50 million are thought to have died from the Spanish flu outbreak, which is more than the number of people who were killed by the war itself.

About 15 000 people died in Australia alone. Our physical distance gave us time to plan and prepare for the onslaught, but we couldn't avoid the health and economic crises that spread across the world. States closed their borders, people had to self-isolate, and strict quarantine measures were imposed. Many events were cancelled, and venues had to close. Public awareness campaigns revolved around good hand hygiene, social distancing and the wearing of face masks. The pandemic came in several waves, and it ended in 1920 when the population finally developed a collective immunity.

Australia was completely spared the effects of the Spanish flu pandemic because we are geographically isolated.

True False

The Spanish flu pandemic seems to have been deadlier than the more recent COVID-19 pandemic.

True False

How did the Spanish flu pandemic end?

a) A vaccine was introduced.

b) Medical treatments cured the disease.

c) The population eventually developed immunity.

d) Another disease took its place.

Social management

4 What questions could you ask a Spanish flu survivor to help you understand what they went through?

____

____

____

This drawing is of an emergency hospital in the United States. The patients are World War I soldiers who were ill with the Spanish flu. Look at the drawing and then answer the questions below.

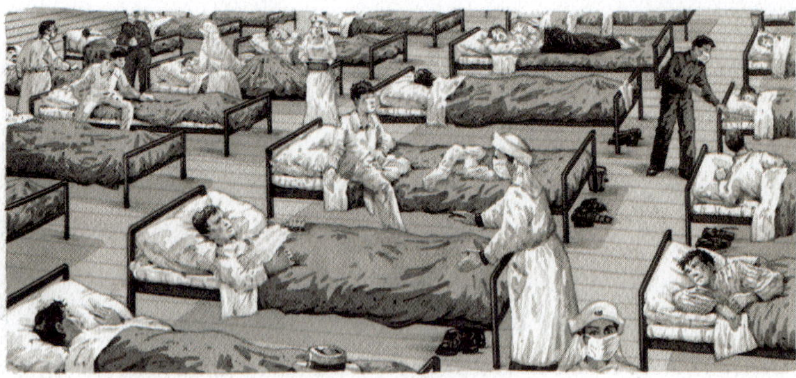

5 Is the photograph what historians call a primary or a secondary source? _______________

6 What does the image tell you about the nature of the illness and the country's state of preparedness for it?

____

____

7 The Spanish flu and COVID-19 led to similar responses by the government in an attempt to control the pandemic. What were these responses?

____

____

Your view

8 Do you think we dealt with COVID-19 better than people dealt with Spanish flu a century ago, or did we fail to learn the lessons of history? Why do you think that?

____

____

HASS – Economics and Business

Australian Curriculum Links: *ACHASSK121, ACHASSK150*

When an economy shrinks, it's said to be in recession. Concern about the financial future makes people nervous and they spend less money. As a result, the demand for goods and services falls. Businesses may start operating at a loss, they invest less, and some businesses fail. People lose their jobs, income levels drop, and consumer spending falls even more.

The worst recession the world faced in the last hundred years was the Great Depression, which was triggered by a stock market crash in 1929. The Global Financial Crisis (GFC) of 2007 was a banking crisis caused by housing loans. Not long after the world recovered from the GFC a new financial crisis struck—this time caused by a virus.

The COVID-19 pandemic impacted global trade as manufacturing plants, first in China and then elsewhere, closed down and/or stopped exporting. Countries quarantined themselves, and tourism levels plummeted. Cafes, gyms and other businesses shut their doors. The Australian government offered financial aid to the millions of people who were affected by the pandemic, increasing support for the unemployed and making payments to businesses to help them keep their staff.

When prices go up, people's willingness to buy products generally ...

a) also goes up.

b) stays the same.

c) goes down.

d) moves around at random.

Which of the following factors influence what a person buys?

a) their taste and personal preferences

b) how much money they have to spend

c) what other people are buying

d) all of the above

Social management

3. What may happen to the economy when people spend less money?

4. At the start of the COVID-19 pandemic, people started panic buying items that they thought would sell out—that is, they bought unusually large quantities. As a result, the items did sell out! What sorts of items did people panic buy?

5. Why is panic buying a problem?

6. The government gave people financial help during the pandemic to try to stop the economy from shrinking too much.

   True False

7. During the pandemic, the government wanted people to save the money they were given, not spend it.

   True False

Your view

8. Was your family financially affected by the COVID-19 pandemic? In what way? Did you receive any financial help, and what form did it take? Did it help you get through?

TARGETING GENERAL CAPABILITIES YEARS 5-6 © PASCAL PRESS ISBN: 9781925726237

Technologies – Design and Technologies

Australian Curriculum Link: *ACTDEK019*

When the COVID-19 pandemic hit, many countries saw a sharp increase in the number of people who required hospitalisation. Thousands of people became extremely ill and needed the support of a special type of medical equipment known as a ventilator—a machine that helps people breathe if they can't breathe on their own. Countries around the world experienced a huge surge in the demand for ventilators. But ventilators are expensive, and they take time to produce. Some countries, including Italy, experienced such extreme shortages that tragically many lives were lost.

Businesses around the world, including in Australia, soon rose to the challenge. New types of ventilators were designed that were cheaper and quicker to produce. Many of these businesses previously produced different products, such as cars or robotic mining equipment, but responded to the market need and switched to designing and developing medical equipment.

1 **Why was there a surge in the demand for ventilators when the COVID-19 pandemic struck?**

____

____

____

____

2 **Do you think it's easy or hard for a hospital to predict the number of ventilators it needs during a pandemic? Why do you think that?**

____

____

____

____

Social management

There was no problem anywhere in the world meeting the increased demand for ventilators.

True False

Designing medical equipment requires skill and expertise.

True False

Designers may be able to adapt their ideas for existing products and use them to create something new.

True False

What do people who design and develop medical equipment need to consider?

a) the costs of production

b) whether the design will work as expected

c) how long the equipment will take to produce

d) all of the above

During a pandemic, why is it helpful if Australian hospitals can buy equipment made locally in Australia?

____

____

____

____

Your view

What do you think is most important during a pandemic crisis: how fast medical equipment can be provided, or how safe and effective it is to use? Explain your answer.

____

____

____

____

TARGETING GENERAL CAPABILITIES YEARS 5-6 © PASCAL PRESS ISBN: 9781925726237

Technologies – Digital Technologies

Australian Curriculum Link: *ACTDIP022*

During the height of the pandemic lockdown, Sophia's school was shut down. She and four of her close friends decided to create their own online isolation diary. That way, they could see what each person was doing every day, even though they couldn't meet in person. They decided to do this through Google Docs.

Sophia set this up by creating a folder inside Google Docs and calling it 'Isolation Diaries'. She then created a document inside the folder called 'Sophia's Diary'. She sent a link to the folder to her four friends' email addresses and told them they should each create a document to use as their own diary. That way, all they needed to do was click the link in their email address once, and they could see each other's diaries in the folder every day. They could even type into and comment on each other's diaries if they wanted to.

With Google Docs, people can only see your document if you send them an email link inviting them to see it.

True False

This means you don't need to be careful with what you put online through Google Docs.

True False

With Google Docs, you can only view other people's information. You are unable to change it in any way.

True False

With Sophia's plan, she and her friends could ...

a) share written information about what they did each day.

b) comment on each other's diaries.

c) share images such as photographs and drawings.

d) all of the above.

Social management

Sophia and her friends wanted to use their diaries interactively in real time, so it felt more like they were actually meeting in person. Suggest a way that they could do that.

Sophia wanted to set some ground rules regarding people's behaviour while writing and commenting on the diaries. What rules can you suggest?

Sophia also wanted to set rules about protecting each other's privacy. After all, they were sharing their personal diaries! What rules can you suggest?

Your view

Assume you and your friends decide to create and share an online diary. What would you use it for? What would you need to do to protect your privacy and that of your friends? What ground rules for behaviour would you set?

Self-reflection

This unit was about social management. What have you learnt about working with others to reach important community goals?

 ISBN: 9781925726237

Self-awareness assessment

This unit was about fads, both past and present. People often join in fads because they feel pressured by their friends or by social media, and they worry about being left out.

Recognise emotions

1. **Think about how you felt when you last took part in a fad: whether it was a game, a dance, or a fashion fad. Write down words that describe how you felt.**

2. **Now write down how you might feel if your friends participate in a fad, but you're not allowed to because your parents disapprove.**

3. **How would your answer to Question 2 change if your parents had a good reason for their disapproval and they explained it to you—for instance, the fad is too expensive or dangerous. Would you feel differently?**

Recognise personal qualities and achievements and develop reflective practice

4. **Fads are all about following the crowd. What sorts of things do you enjoy doing simply because you like them, not because other people tell you that you should like them?**

Understand self as learner

There are different learning styles to suit people who have different work habits. These different styles of learning include:

- seeing learners – who like to see images
- hearing learners – who like to hear explanations
- writing learners – who like to read texts
- doing learners – who learn best by doing things.

The list below shows different work preferences and habits. Put them in the right places in the table.

Read book   Listen to teacher   Look at diagrams

Listen to podcast   Look at infographics   Follow demonstration

Write notes   Perform experiment

Seeing learners	Hearing learners	Writing learners	Doing learners

6 Which type of learner are you? Which work habits will suit you best?

____

____

____

____

____

____

____

____

TARGETING GENERAL CAPABILITIES YEARS 5-6 © PASCAL PRESS ISBN: 9781925726237

Self-management assessment

This unit was about kitchen gardens and scarecrows, but it was also about working hard to achieve your goals.

Express emotions appropriately

1. How do you feel when you achieve one of your goals?

____

____

____

____

____

____

2. How do you feel when you work hard at a goal, but then realise it was more difficult than you first expected?

____

____

____

____

____

____

3. Do you become more determined to succeed when things are hard, or are you more likely to give up? What do you consider when making such decisions?

____

____

____

____

____

____

Develop self-discipline and set goals

When setting your goals, it's a good idea to divide them into short-, medium- and long-term goals. This makes them more realistic and easier to manage.

Look at Joseph's goals listed below. Are they short, medium or long term? Put them in the right places in the table.

finish homework   pass end-of-term exams   go to friend's house
practise piano   become a doctor   live near the beach
learn a new instrument   learn another language   travel the world

Short-term goals	Medium-term goals	Long-term goals

What about your own goals? Divide them into short, medium and long term, and write them in the table.

Short-term goals	Medium-term goals	Long-term goals

Work independently and show initiative

Teamwork is important, but it's also often necessary to be able to work independently.

Discuss why Faruq took initiative to build a scarecrow in Unit 2 and how he managed to work independently to reach his goal.

____

____

Become confident, resilient and adaptable

Look at the words and phrases below. Circle the ones that you think can help people to achieve challenging tasks.

give up   get upset   keep trying   blame someone
be positive   ask for help   say it's too hard   take a chance
learn more   throw a tantrum   enjoy the process   cry

TARGETING GENERAL CAPABILITIES YEARS 5-6 © PASCAL PRESS ISBN: 9781925726237

Social awareness assessment

This unit was about the different views that people in society have about climate change. Most people agree it's a serious issue, but some people do not. Even people who agree it's a problem can disagree over what should be done about it. Calm communication can help people understand each other's point of view.

Appreciate diverse perspectives

1. **Five different people were quoted in the article on page 29, expressing their views about climate change in general and about the climate strikes in particular. What were their views? Fill in the table below with the responses YES or NO.**

Who?	Concerned about climate change	Support climate strikes
Dylan Miller		
Ming Chan		
John Kowalski		
Camilla Smythe		
Robin Voyle		

2. **What are some reasons people give for supporting the climate strikes?**

____

____

____

____

3. **What are some reasons people give for NOT supporting the climate strikes?**

____

____

____

____

ASSESSMENT

The way you express your ideas can either help others understand your viewpoint, or it can make it more difficult. Do you think the way each person in the article expressed themselves helped or hindered other people's understanding? Why?

i. Dylan Miller ______________________

ii. Ming Chan ______________________

iii. John Kowalski ______________________

iv. Camilla Smythe ______________________

v. Robin Voyle ______________________

Contribute to civil society

There are several ways we can take action to address community needs or problems. Pick the approach you think would work best to tackle climate change.

community meeting | climate awareness leaflet | vote for new laws

Explain why you chose this method.

____

____

____

Understand relationships

Many factors contribute to positive community relationships. Use words from the word bank to find things that are positive and things that are negative. Fill in the table.

Word bank

discussing | ignoring | sarcasm | listening | applauding
interrupting | patience | shouting | taking turns | booing

Positive effect	Negative effect

TARGETING GENERAL CAPABILITIES YEARS 5-6 © PASCAL PRESS ISBN: 9781925726237

Social management assessment

Communicate effectively and work collaboratively

This unit was about the need for people to work together to meet important communal goals and the issues that can arise when people have differing viewpoints.

1. **Read the Premier's media release on page 40. The Premier wanted people to follow the new rules imposed during the COVID-19 pandemic and wear face masks when out in public. Write a short speech aimed at your classmates, encouraging them to wear masks and help stop the spread of a disease.**

____

____

____

____

____

____

Make decisions

2. **What sorts of things do you think the government considered when passing laws that forced people to wear face coverings when out in public?**

____

____

____

____

3. **Did the government face competing considerations? What were they?**

____

____

____

____

Negotiate and resolve conflict

The government's rules caused conflict in society. Some people thought that wearing face coverings was a sensible precaution, others believed it was unnecessary and placed an unreasonable restriction on people's freedom. It isn't always possible to avoid disagreements, but there are things we can do to identify the causes of conflict and work towards a solution.

4 Unjumble the words in the sentences below to discover what they are. The first letter of each word is given to you.

i. It is important to **pexilan** the reasons for a decision. e________

ii. People should have the chance to **ltka** about how they feel. t________

iii. It is important to **tselin** to different points of view. l________

iv. Even if we disagree, we should still **repetsc** other's views. r________

v. The aim is to find a solution that **toms** people are happy with. m________

Develop leadership skills

Children aged under 12 didn't have to wear face coverings under the COVID-19 pandemic laws. However, assume that everyone in your school DOES now have to wear a face mask due to the outbreak of a new disease. Some children are happy to wear masks, others are not. You decide to help resolve the conflict. Write down some steps that you might take.

____

____

____

____

____

____

____

____

____

TARGETING GENERAL CAPABILITIES YEARS 5-6 © PASCAL PRESS ISBN: 9781925726237

Intercultural Understanding

Intercultural understanding encourages children to be aware of the importance of becoming responsible global citizens by enhancing cultural knowledge. As outlined in the curriculum, the elements and sub-elements are:

Recognising culture and developing respect: investigate culture and cultural identity; explore and compare cultural knowledge, beliefs and practices; develop respect for cultural diversity

Interacting and empathising with others: communicate across cultures; consider and develop multiple perspectives; empathise with others

Reflecting on intercultural experiences and taking responsibility: reflect on intercultural experiences; challenge stereotypes and prejudices; mediate cultural difference.

REASONS FOR MIGRATION IN THE 20TH CENTURY

The word migrate means to 'move from one place to another'. During the 20th century, people migrated to and from Australia for many different reasons. These reasons are called push and pull factors.

Events that 'pushed' people to Australia in the 1900s

Wars: Many people were pushed out of their homelands in Europe because of World War II. After the war, they were unable or unwilling to return to their homelands and were forced to live in refugee camps. These people became known as 'displaced persons'. Australia wanted to increase its population, so the government agreed to resettle many of these people.

Religious Persecution: People who are forced out of their countries because of their religion are called religious refugees. Jewish people were pushed out of Germany in the 1930s and 1940s because of unfair and poor treatment, known as religious persecution. Many were forced to flee, often with no money and no possessions. Australia agreed to accept some of these religious refugees.

Laws and Government Policies: Sometimes governments make laws that make life difficult for people. After Federation in 1901, the government created laws known as the White Australia Policy. These were meant to create a mostly white and British population. Many non-British people were pushed out of Australia through deportation.

Push factors are things that 'push' people out of a country, while pull factors are things that 'pull' people towards a country. These factors are often significant events, such as wars or laws and policies made by a country's government.

Events that 'pulled' people to Australia in the 1900s

Work Opportunities: The Snowy Mountains Scheme in New South Wales was a project that needed a very large workforce. Australia did not have many people with the required skills to build the project. Many experienced migrants from Europe were pulled to Australia to work on the scheme, as well as those who came because they were drawn by the high wages.

Better Quality of Life: Many people believed Australia offered them a better way of life than that of their own countries. As Australia was a young and developing country, many people, particularly those from Britain and Ireland, were pulled to Australia by the warm weather and the possibilities of better jobs and owning a home.

Laws and Government Policies: Sometimes governments make laws and policies that encourage certain people to migrate to a country. Although the White Australia Policy pushed many non-British people out of Australia, it also pulled people from the United Kingdom and Ireland to the country. The government also provided cheap passage on ships and services to help people settle when they arrived.

Source: *Australian History Centres: Upper Primary, p.61, Blake Education*

English – Literacy

Australian Curriculum Links: *ACELY1701, ACELY1712*

Texts can be written, spoken or multimodal. A 'multimodal' text combines different forms of communication, for instance print text, visual images and/or sound. The written text on the previous page is accompanied by pictures of two multimodal texts (right). These are posters that include both print text and visual images.

Read the written text on page 60, look at the two posters above and answer the following questions.

1 The written text is a type of __________ text.

a) imaginative b) informative c) persuasive d) multimodal

2 What is the purpose of the written text?

____

____

3 How is the written text structured?

a) headings and paragraphs c) dialogue

b) bullet points d) chronological steps

4 Does the structure of the written text make the material easy to follow and understand? Explain your answer.

____

____

5 **What is the purpose of the two posters?**

a) to explain why people migrated to Australia in the 1900s

b) to encourage people to migrate to Australia

c) to impose the White Australia Policy

d) to illustrate the difference between 'push' and 'pull' factors

6 **Look at the first poster, titled 'Australia land of tomorrow'. How would you describe it? What image of Australia is it trying to portray?**

___

___

7 **Look at the second poster. How does it differ from the first? Why do you think it is so different?**

Hint: Think about whether it might have been created for a different audience.

___

___

Your turn

8 **You've been asked to design a poster to encourage people to migrate to Australia in the 21st century. Consider and answer the following:**

i. Who is your audience?

___

ii. What image of Australia do you want to portray?

___

iii. What balance do you want between print text and images?

___

iv. What will the print text say?

___

Draw a sketch of your poster.

TARGETING GENERAL CAPABILITIES YEARS 5-6 © PASCAL PRESS ISBN: 9781925726237

HASS – History

Australian Curriculum Links: *ACHASSK109, ACHASSK136*

SPONSOR A SKILLED MIGRANT

To: COMMONWEALTH MIGRATION OFFICER,

I wish to suggest Mr. VASILIOS YIOUVANTZIS as a possible migrant to Australia. His personal particulars are set out below:—

(1) Family Name ① YIOUVANTZIS (Block letters) Given Name ② VASILIOS

(2) Address ③ GREECE (Country) ④ XANTHE (City ~~or Province~~)

~~(Suburb or Village)~~ ⑤ LEONTOS SOFOU (Street) 8 (No.)

(3) Nationality ⑥ Greek (4) Place and Date of Birth ⑦ KALYFITON - DRAMA - GREECE, 1931? (or approximate age)

(5) He is a skilled tradesman in the occupation of ⑧ Oxy + Electric welder

(6) His qualifications and experience in that occupation are ⑨ Oxy and ELECTRIC ? WELDER

(7) Relationship to me ⑩ WIFE'S BROTHER (8) His Marital Status ⑪ MARRIED

(9) Given Name of his Wife ⑫ GEORGIA ? (10) Number of Children ⑬ TWO

(11) ⑭ He would/~~would not~~ wish to be accompanied by his wife and children.

(12) I can/~~cannot~~ arrange accommodation.

(13) My name is TARAKZOGLOU Constantine

(14) My address is 71 Lawson St Bondi Junction NSW

FOR OFFICIAL USE

Date 21 July 1963 , Signature

The text on page 60 is about the reasons that people migrated to Australia in the 20th century. Read the text, look at the document above, and answer the following questions.

Explain the difference between migration 'push' and 'pull' factors.

____

____

Which of the following events did NOT push people out of Europe in the 1900s?

a) World War II

b) religious persecution

c) poverty

d) the White Australia Policy

3 **What pulled people to Australia in the 1900s?**

a) work opportunities

b) quality of life

c) climate

d) all of the above

4 **Why do you think the Australian government wanted to increase the country's population?**

____

____

5 **Look at the document on the previous page. Would historians call this a primary or a secondary source?**

____

6 **The document is an application to sponsor a skilled migrant. Which country did the potential migrant live in?**

____

7 **Why do you think the potential migrant wanted to move to Australia?**

____

____

Your turn

8 **Does your family have a migration story? Who was the first to arrive in Australia and when did they come? Why did they come to Australia? Find out as much as you can, write it down and share it with the rest of your class.**

____

____

____

____

TARGETING GENERAL CAPABILITIES YEARS 5-6 © PASCAL PRESS ISBN: 9781925726237

HASS – Geography

Australian Curriculum Links: *ACHASSK113, ACHASSK140*

The Australian Bureau of Statistics (ABS) collects census data every five years. It collects information about the population that provides a detailed snapshot of who we are. One of the things it looks at is the cultural diversity of our population and where migrants are most likely to live. The 2016 census found that Sydney had the largest overseas-born population, followed by Melbourne and then Perth. It also found that 83 per cent of people born overseas lived in a capital city, compared to only 61 per cent of the Australian-born population.

The following table looks at where our overseas population comes from and compares figures from the 2011 and 2016 censuses. Look at the table and answer the questions below.

OVERSEAS COUNTRY OF BIRTH BY REGION, 2011 AND 2016

	2011		2016	
Region of birth	**Persons**	**Proportion of overseas-born population %**	**Persons**	**Proportion of overseas-born population %**
North-West Europe	1 441 874	27.3	1 431 169	23.2
South-East Asia	701 863	13.3	872 891	14.2
North-East Asia	535 483	10.1	789 436	12.8
Southern and Central Asia	500 743	9.5	782 903	12.7
Southern and Eastern Europe	689 179	13.0	657 698	10.7
Oceania and Antarctica(a)	609 158	11.5	657 696	10.7
Sub-Saharan Africa	272 519	5.2	317 182	5.1
Middle East	240 442	4.5	303 089	4.9
Northern America	116 419	2.2	129 704	2.1
South America	87 676	1.7	114 599	1.9
Other Americas(b)	19 646	0.4	21 751	0.4
North Africa	65 307	1.2	70 994	1.2
Total(c)	**5 290 203**	**100**	**6 163 667**	**100**

(a) Excludes those born in Australia.

(b) Other Americas includes Central America, Caribbean and Americas, nfd.

(c) Total includes Inadequately described, At sea, and North Africa and the Middle East, nfd.

Source: Census of Population and Housing 2011, 2016

Source: https://www.abs.gov.au/ausstats/abs@.nsf/Latestproducts/2071.0Main%20Features602016?opendocument&tabname=Summary&prodno=2071.0&issue=2016&num=&view=

Which region do most overseas-born Australians come from?

____

Recognising culture & developing respect

Has the proportion of people born in North-West Europe increased from 2011 to 2016 or decreased?

___

Find two regions where the proportion has remained the same in both censuses.

i. ___ ii. ___

There has been an increase in the number of Australians who were born in ...

a) Asia. b) the Middle East. c) South America. d) all of the above.

Overseas-born Australians are more likely than the local-born to live in a capital city.

True False

Most capital cities throughout Australia are inland, far from the coast.

True False

Why do you think migrants tend to be drawn to capital cities?

___

___

Your turn

8 **Were any of your classmates or their families born overseas? Do a headcount and record the following information:**

- How many people in your class were born overseas? ___
- How many people in your class were born in Australia? ___
- Of those born in Australia, how many have one or more parent born overseas? ___
- List all the countries of birth of your classmates and their families.

___

INTERCULTURAL UNDERSTANDING

TARGETING GENERAL CAPABILITIES YEARS 5-6 © PASCAL PRESS ISBN: 9781925726237

The Arts – Dance

Australian Curriculum Links: *ACADAM011, ACADAR012*

Bollywood dancing is known throughout the world, spread by India's film industry. Bollywood is a fusion of different Indian dance moves, including the more traditional bhangra, a folk-dance originating in the Punjab. The more recent films combine Western choreography with traditional movements, demonstrating that the Bollywood style of dancing is continually evolving to suit its growing and diverse audience.

"Bollywood at The High" by TimothyJ is licensed under CC BY 2.0
Source: https://search.creativecommons.org/photos/2ec5fe77-df00-41fe-b288-0497ae018c12

Many cultures use dance as a way of celebrating and communicating their identity. It can be easier to understand a performance if you break the dance down into four basic elements:

i. Space

Space refers to the pattern a dancer makes as they move, be it sideways, forwards, backwards or diagonal. They can be up high or down low. They can keep both feet on the floor, raise one foot and leap. They can face the audience or turn away.

ii. Time

A dance can be fast, slow or anything in between. It can be continuous or there can be pauses. Like music, dance has a rhythm.

iii. Dynamics

Dynamics refers to the energy level of the performance. It can be high or low, gentle or strong. Movements can be flowing or sharp, wobbly or stiff.

iv. Relationships

Dancers can dance alone or in a group. They can come together or move apart. They can reflect each other's movements, or they can perform different moves.

Recognising culture & developing respect

INTERCULTURAL UNDERSTANDING

Look at the image on page 67 and answer the following questions.

1. Bollywood films have spread Indian music, dance and culture to other countries including Australia.

   True False

2. People who enjoy the films and music of a cultural group often want to learn more about the culture.

   True False

3. List the four elements of dance.

   ____

4. Are the dancers in the picture up high or keeping low to the ground? What do you think this might indicate?

   ____

   ____

5. By looking at the image, would you expect this to be a fast or slow dance? What makes you think that?

   ____

   ____

6. How would you describe the relationship of the dancers?

   ____

   ____

7. Apart from dance, list other things that different cultures have brought to Australia that we can all enjoy and benefit from.

   ____

   ____

Your turn

8. It isn't easy to study a dance by looking at a still image—you need to see it in motion. Find a video of a Bollywood dance performance and analyse it in terms of the four elements.

   ____

   ____

   ____

TARGETING GENERAL CAPABILITIES YEARS 5-6 © PASCAL PRESS ISBN: 9781925726237

Health & Physical Education

Australian Curriculum Links: *ACPPS051, ACPPS060*

Source: https://www.ceh.org.au/harmony-day-march-on/

Harmony Day falls on 21 March each year, and it coincides with the United Nations' International Day for the Elimination of Racial Discrimination. The message is 'Everyone Belongs', and it's a chance to celebrate the diverse cultures that make up modern-day Australia.

In 2019, Harmony Day was extended to a week, allowing more time for the activities that celebrate diversity. These activities include the sharing of music, art, dance, films, sport and food. They are held by schools, businesses and government bodies as well as community, sports and religious groups all across the nation. The official colour for Harmony Day is orange, and people are encouraged to show their support by wearing something orange.

 **Why is Harmony Day held on 21 March each year?**

____

 **What is the ongoing message behind Harmony Day?**

____

 **How does the banner above reinforce the message of Harmony Day?**

____

____

INTERCULTURAL UNDERSTANDING

A person's sense of identity comes from ...

a) where they come from.

b) where they feel they belong.

c) who they relate to.

d) all of the above.

Suggest some possible reasons why orange was chosen as the official colour for Harmony Day.

What problems can arise in society when people of diverse cultures are made to feel that they don't belong?

How can valuing cultural diversity benefit the wellbeing of the broader community?

Your turn

Imagine your school is planning a Harmony Week event that celebrates diversity and you are asked to contribute something from your own culture to share with others. What would you bring and why?

Self-reflection

This unit was about recognising culture and developing respect. What have you learnt about respecting the traditions of other cultures in multicultural Australia?

TARGETING GENERAL CAPABILITIES YEARS 5-6 © PASCAL PRESS ISBN: 9781925726237

ULURU

Right in the middle of Australia stands a huge red rock—Uluru.

The rock and the country around it belong to a group of Aboriginal people called Pitjantjatjara and Yankunytjatjara. They are very difficult words, so they say, call us Anangu (The People).

Anangu have lived here for tens of thousands of years. They are connected to their land, the plants and the animals through Tjukurpa. Tjukurpa is many things. It is the time of creation when heroic ancestral beings made the land. It is the law that governs and guides all the people's actions. It is the life force joining the people to the natural world. Ceremony and sacred places make the people one with Tjukurpa.

Because of Tjukurpa, Anangu know their lands so well that they can always find food and water, even during drought.

They lived well in good times. More importantly, they survived in the harshest years, even in the days before they owned cars or had a supermarket to shop at. Everything they needed for body and spirit they found in the land.

Anangu own the land, but they know that this place is important to other Australians as well, and they are very happy to share it with visitors from all over the world. More than 400 000 visitors come every year. Anangu generously share much of their culture with all of these visitors. Tony Tjamiwa says, 'Our purpose is to explain and clarify our understanding of our world so that others can understand.'

An important part of Anangu law is that people should not climb the rock—Uluru. To Anangu it is a sacred place. In fact, on 25 October 2019, the climb up Uluru was permanently closed. Thirty-four years after the Anangu people were given back the title to the land, their desire to keep people off the rock will be enforced by law. Instead of climbing Uluru, Anangu urge visitors to go on the Mala (wallaby) and Liru (snake) walks, which are guided by Anangu and other rangers.

Through their parents, grandparents, aunts and uncles, Anangu children learn about Tjukurpa. They learn the songs and dances for inma (ceremonies). The girls are painted for the Kuniya (python) and the boys act the story of Lungkata, the blue-tongued lizard. The stories told come from the creative time. It is Anangu's duty to look after Tjukurpa. The elders say, 'It provides us with our reason for living. Our law is how it should be.' Inma are important; they teach young people to keep the Law properly in their hearts and minds.

Source: Sharing Culture: *Uluru*, pp.1–2, p.18, p.53, Steve Parish

INTERCULTURAL UNDERSTANDING

English – Language

Australian Curriculum Links: *ACELA1501, ACELA1515*

Not all Australians speak in the same way. Most countries around the world have different social or geographical dialects and accents, and Australia is no exception. Standard Australian English is the formal way of talking for official and public purposes, but there are also many types of informal ways of speaking, and these can differ across regions. In addition, there are more than 150 Aboriginal languages and two Torres Strait Islander languages spoken, and they relate to different geographical areas.

Read the article on page 71 and answer the following questions.

What type of text is the article?

a) informative

b) persuasive

c) imaginative

d) all of the above

Why do the Pitjantjatjara and Yankunytjatjara people ask to be called 'Anangu', and what does it mean?

____

____

In the article, Anangu member Tony Tjamiwa says, 'Our purpose is to explain and clarify our understanding of our world so that others can understand.' The language as used in this quote is most likely ...

a) an Aboriginal language or dialect.

b) Standard Australian English.

c) informal talk between close friends.

d) Australian slang particular to the Uluru region.

TARGETING GENERAL CAPABILITIES YEARS 5-6 © PASCAL PRESS ISBN: 9781925726237

Who was Tony Tjamiwa addressing with his comments?

a) members of his family

b) the general public

c) some strangers he met in an informal social setting

d) a historian documenting Uluru's history

5 Why do you think he spoke in this manner?

____

____

____

____

All different languages, dialects and accents are of equal value.

True False

People belonging to different cultures may speak in different ways, including periods of silence and levels of formality.

True False

Your view

How would you ask people to understand and respect your culture? Write a few sentences asking people to understand something that is important to your culture.

Hint: Think about the things that matter to you and your family, for instance your way of dressing, any dietary restrictions, your religious beliefs and celebrations, etc.

____

____

____

____

HASS – Civics and Citizenship

Australian Curriculum Links: *ACHASSK118, ACHASSK146*

Uluru, once known as Ayers Rock, has been sacred to the Anangu people for tens of thousands of years. Under their law and culture, climbing the rock was generally not permitted. However, non-Indigenous visitors began climbing Uluru as a tourist activity as far back as the 1930s.

In 1985, the Uluru-Kata Tjuta National Park was handed back to the traditional people. Although it was still legal to climb the rock, the Anangu people asked visitors to respect their culture and their wishes, and to stop climbing. Numbers slowly dropped as visitors learnt more about the Anangu culture. Finally, in 2019, a law was passed prohibiting visitors from climbing Uluru. Attempting to climb it is now a breach of the *Environmental Protection and Biodiversity Act 1999* and can result in the imposition of a penalty.

Why did the Anangu people ask visitors not to climb Uluru?

a) It was against their sacred beliefs.

b) It was too dangerous.

c) It threatened endangered species.

d) It was a breach of the *Environmental Protection and Biodiversity Act*.

All visitors immediately stopped climbing Uluru when the Anangu people asked them to respect their wishes.

True False

Government legislation was needed to enforce the wishes of the Anangu people.

True False

TARGETING GENERAL CAPABILITIES YEARS 5-6 © PASCAL PRESS ISBN: 9781925726237

4 **Where might the idea for the 2019 law have come from?**

a) a request by the Anangu people

b) pressure from people sympathetic to the Anangu's wishes

c) tourism operators who run rock-climbing tours

d) both a and b

Use words from the word bank to complete the cloze passages.

Word bank

law lobby committee

5 **People with shared beliefs and values can join together and ________ the government to change an unfair law.**

6 **Parliament can set up a ____________ to examine an issue, and they may suggest that a bill or proposed law be introduced.**

7 **For a bill to become a __________, it needs to be voted on by parliament.**

Your view

8 **Not everybody was supportive of the laws that prohibited climbing Uluru. Based on what you have read above and the articles about Uluru, what would you say to them?**

____

____

____

____

HASS – Geography

Australian Curriculum Links: *ACHASSK112, ACHASSK140*

Indigenous Australian peoples, like many indigenous cultures around the world, traditionally relied upon the environment to provide everything they needed to live and thrive. For this reason, they learned to sustainably use the resources available. This means they managed their environment in ways that kept it healthy so that it could provide for them for generations to come. This is how they achieved it.

Moved with the seasons

Some Indigenous Australian groups moved seasonally from area to area as the amount of food varied throughout the year. This provided them with a continuous supply of food and enabled food sources to re-establish before being harvested again.

Lived by the patterns of nature

Over thousands of years, Indigenous Australian peoples observed the land and its animals and plants. They became familiar with the seasons and knew that with each season came change. Some seasons were better for hunting or fishing, while others were better for collecting fruits and vegetables or for preparing medicines. They planned their lives around the cycles of nature.

Used a wide variety of plants and animals

They understood that all forms of nature, including humans, depend on each other for survival. They used a wide variety of plants and animals to ensure the supply of any one plant or animal never ran out, avoiding any knock-on effects. They took only what they needed from the land and never wasted anything.

Fire-stick farming

They used fire in a sustainable manner to make the environment more suitable for humans. They did this by regularly burning small patches over large areas. This limited the intensity of large bushfires as there was less to burn. In addition, the regrowth after the fire attracted animals, which could be hunted as they fed off the fresh green shoots. The burning created a pasture-like landscape, which made it easier to move and hunt.

Shared knowledge

They passed down the knowledge of how to live a sustainable life, and the importance of doing so, to the younger generations through stories, song, art and dance.

Source: Australian Geography Centres: Upper Primary, p.51, Blake Education

TARGETING GENERAL CAPABILITIES YEARS 5-6 © PASCAL PRESS ISBN: 9781925726237

1 What does 'sustainability' mean?

2 How did observing the seasons allow Indigenous Australians to live a sustainable lifestyle?

3 Indigenous people have long understood that all elements of nature depend on each other for survival.

True False

4 Sustainable practices involve taking more than is needed, resulting in significant wastage.

True False

5 Explain what is meant by a 'knock-on effect'?

6 How has fire-stick farming physically altered the environment?

7 How did fire-stick farming help Indigenous people live sustainably?

Your view

8 The Anangu people are happy to share their knowledge about their land with visitors from other parts of Australia and from all around the world. Write down a list of questions that you would like to ask them if you had the opportunity to visit.

Interacting & empathising with others

Science

Australian Curriculum Links: *ACSSU043, ACSSU094*

For tens of thousands of years, Indigenous Australians have understood that plant and animal species are adapted to their environment, and that their growth and survival is affected by the physical conditions around them. By studying the weather patterns and how the environment changes with the seasons, Indigenous Australians were able to live in harmony with their land and manage it sustainably.

In 2002, an Indigenous Weather Knowledge website was set up between the Bureau of Meteorology, the Aboriginal and Torres Strait Islander Commission (ATSIC), and Monash University's Centre for Indigenous Studies. It shares the traditional weather and climate knowledge that has been passed down over many generations.

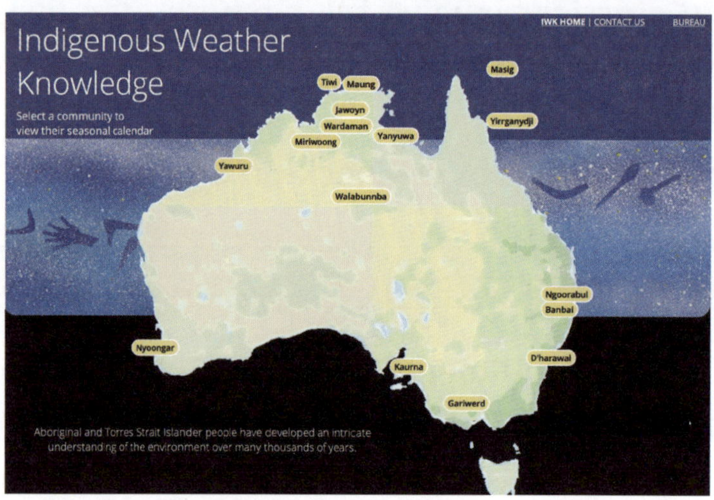

Source: http://www.bom.gov.au/iwk/index.shtml

The website displays a map of Australia, labelled with different Indigenous communities. By clicking on the name of the community, you can see an explanation of their calendar and seasons.

For instance, in D'harawal Country, which stretches from Sydney Harbour to the Shoalhaven River, six seasons have been identified. They are:

- Burran – hot and dry (January to March)
- Marrai'gang – wet becoming cool (April to June)
- Burrugin – cold and frosty (June and July)
- Wiritjiribin – cold and windy (July and August)
- Ngoonungi – cool becoming warm (September and October)
- Parra'dowee – warm and wet (November and December).

Each description contains seasonal observations, for instance, when lilly pillies ripen, when lyrebirds build mounds and when gentle rain is expected.

Interacting & empathising with others

INTERCULTURAL UNDERSTANDING

Indigenous Australians lived in harmony with the land by ...

a) studying weather patterns.

b) observing how the environment changes with the seasons.

c) understanding the effect of the climate on plants and animals.

d) all of the above.

Who set up the Indigenous Weather Knowledge website and why?

___

Indigenous seasons are the same as European people's ideas of seasons.

True False

Indigenous seasons are more likely to reflect the real, observed local environment than the imported European notion of seasons.

True False

Indigenous seasons are defined by both, temperatures and likely precipitation.

True False

Which provides more detail of the expected weather in a given month, Indigenous or imported seasons? Explain your answer.

___

___

The time of Parra'dowee is the time when the native plant Kai'arrewan (coastal wattle) flowers. Why might this be important to the local people?

a) They like the look of the flowers.

b) The plant is dangerous and should be avoided.

c) It signals that at this time, there will be fish in the bays and estuaries.

d) all of the above

Go to the Indigenous Weather Knowledge map at http://www.bom.gov.au/iwk/index.shtml. Find the Indigenous community closest to your home and click on it. Write a brief summary of the calendar and seasons. What new things has this taught you about the area in which you live?

___

___

TARGETING GENERAL CAPABILITIES YEARS 5-6 © PASCAL PRESS ISBN: 9781925726237

Technologies – Design and Technologies

Australian Curriculum Link: *ACTDEK019*

People in design and technologies occupations often face competing considerations when designing products, services or environmental solutions. This has certainly been the case for tour operators at Uluru. Visitors were allowed to climb the rock until recent years, when legislation banned it. Climbing the rock may have benefited tourists and tour group organisers, but it upset the Anangu people who saw it as a violation of their sacred beliefs.

In many countries, including Australia, the development of the tourism industry has seen the forced removal of Indigenous people from their traditional lands. Some are even prevented from returning and do not benefit from the revenue the tourism generates.

The best way to protect the Indigenous community is to involve them in the plans. They should have a say in how their land is used and can benefit from the increased job opportunities and tourist money that enters the community. This also benefits tourists as they get to enjoy an authentic cultural experience.

Read the above plus the article on page 71 and answer the questions.

People who work in design and technologies occupations often have to deal with competing considerations.

True False

Tour and travel service planners need to consider ...

a) the financial cost of their services.

b) any impacts on the environment.

c) any impacts on Indigenous communities.

d) all of the above.

In the case of tours to Uluru, which groups were the competing considerations between?

____

TARGETING GENERAL CAPABILITIES YEARS 5-6 © PASCAL PRESS ISBN: 9781925726237

4 Why do you think the Anangu people are happy to share their land with visitors?

5 What is the best way to both, protect Indigenous people and offer tourists a good holiday experience?

6 It took 34 years from the time the Anangu were given land rights to the time their wishes regarding climbing Uluru were recognised and enforced by law. Why do you think it took so long?

7 Do the Anangu people offer other tour options to visitors? What are they?

Your turn

8 Have you visited a site of Indigenous cultural importance in Australia? What was it? What did you learn there?

Self-reflection

This unit was about interacting and empathising with others. What have you learnt about the importance of understanding people from different cultures?

Indigenous Rights

The Constitution

Aboriginal peoples were only mentioned twice in the 1901 Australian Constitution, and Torres Strait Islander peoples were not mentioned at all. Indigenous peoples were also not counted in the census and were often viewed as second-class citizens, so they did not receive the same rights and freedoms as other Australians. They were even looked after by the same department that dealt with national parks, flora and fauna.

Full Control

Only the newly formed states could make laws that applied to Aboriginal peoples. As colonies, most states had Aboriginal Protection Boards and roles such as Protector of Aborigines. These were meant to protect Aboriginal peoples, but they actually controlled their lives. They were required to ask the Protector for permission to marry, move, travel and even to access their wages. The states controlled whom they could work for, how much they got paid, their education, housing and more.

Citizenship

In 1948, the *Nationality and Citizenship Act* was passed. This Act meant that all people born in Australia were classified as Australian citizens, including Aboriginal and Torres Strait Islander peoples. Anyone who was an Australian citizen was also considered a British subject.

Right to Vote

Although they were considered Australian citizens, Indigenous peoples still did not have the right to vote. In 1961, a Commonwealth Parliamentary Committee investigated and reported on Indigenous voting rights. This resulted in amendments to the *Commonwealth Electoral Act* in 1962, which allowed Indigenous peoples to enrol to vote in federal elections if they wished. It was not compulsory for Indigenous peoples to enrol to vote, unlike other Australians.

Referendum

In 1967, a national referendum was held. Australians were asked if they agreed that Indigenous peoples should be counted in the census and that the Commonwealth Government could pass laws for Indigenous peoples. More than 90 per cent of Australians voted 'yes'. The Constitution was amended to include these changes.

Source: *Blake's Australian History Guide*, p.77, Pascal Press

English – Literacy

Australian Curriculum Links: *ACELY1703, ACELY1713*

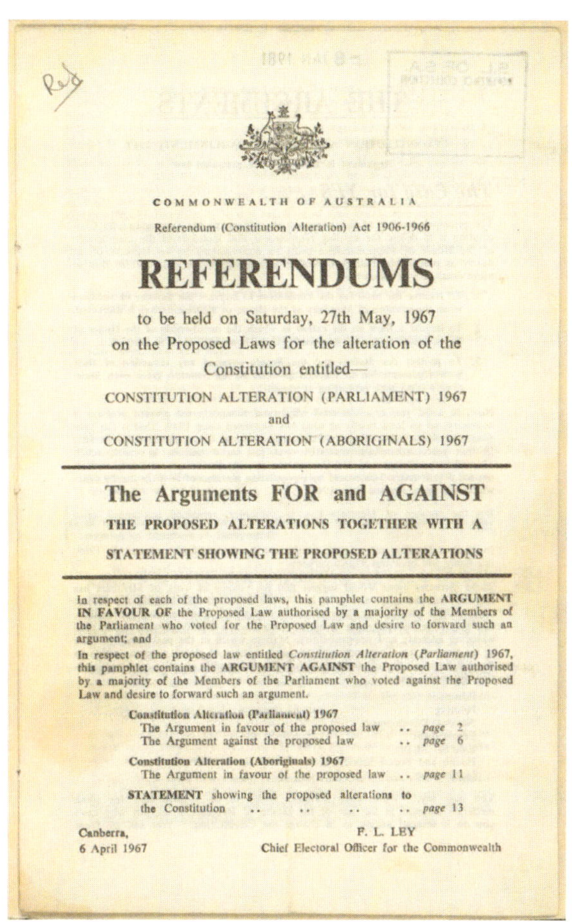

COMMONWEALTH OF AUSTRALIA

Referendum (Constitution Alteration) Act 1906-1966

REFERENDUMS

to be held on Saturday, 27th May, 1967
on the Proposed Laws for the alteration of the
Constitution entitled—

CONSTITUTION ALTERATION (PARLIAMENT) 1967
and
CONSTITUTION ALTERATION (ABORIGINALS) 1967

The Arguments FOR and AGAINST
THE PROPOSED ALTERATIONS TOGETHER WITH A STATEMENT SHOWING THE PROPOSED ALTERATIONS

In respect of each of the proposed laws, this pamphlet contains the **ARGUMENT IN FAVOUR OF** the Proposed Law authorised by a majority of the Members of the Parliament who voted for the Proposed Law and desire to forward such an argument; and

In respect of the proposed law entitled *Constitution Alteration (Parliament)* 1967, this pamphlet contains the **ARGUMENT AGAINST** the Proposed Law authorised by a majority of the Members of the Parliament who voted against the Proposed Law and desire to forward such an argument.

Constitution Alteration (Parliament) 1967
The Argument in favour of the proposed law .. *page* 2
The Argument against the proposed law .. *page* 6

Constitution Alteration (Aboriginals) 1967
The Argument in favour of the proposed law .. *page* 11

STATEMENT showing the proposed alterations to the Constitution .. .. *page* 13

Canberra,
6 April 1967

F. L. LEY
Chief Electoral Officer for the Commonwealth

Read the article on page 82, examine the image above, and answer the following questions.

In which year did the Australian Constitution come into effect?

____

How many times were ...

i. Aboriginal peoples mentioned in the original version of the constitution? ____________

ii. Torres Strait Islanders mentioned in the original version of the constitution? ____________

Reflecting on intercultural experiences & taking responsibility

At the time of Federation, who could pass laws regarding Indigenous Australians?

a) the Commonwealth government

b) the colonies

c) the newly formed states

d) all of the above

INTERCULTURAL UNDERSTANDING

What was the role of the Aboriginal Protection Boards, and what did they actually do?

In which year were Indigenous Australians permitted to vote in federal elections?

a) 1900

b) 1948

c) 1962

d) 1967

The image on page 83 shows the first page of a document published in 1967. Judging by what is written on this page, what information does the document contain?

Where could you look if you wanted to read the above document in its entirety?

Your turn

Write a list of questions you could ask to find out more about the 1967 constitutional reforms.

TARGETING GENERAL CAPABILITIES YEARS 5-6 © PASCAL PRESS ISBN: 9781925726237

HASS – Civics and Citizenship

Australian Curriculum Links: *ACHASSK116, ACHASSK145*

VOTING

All Australian citizens aged 18 and over must enrol to vote, and voting is compulsory for federal, state and local elections. This wasn't always the case, however. The minimum voting age was 21 up until 1973, and Australian women weren't able to vote at all until the late 1890s or the early 1900s, depending on where they lived. Indigenous Australians couldn't vote in federal elections until 1962, and it wasn't until as recently as 1983 that they were actually required to vote, finally removing the racial distinction.

Australians vote by participating in a secret ballot, meaning that nobody is able to see who they have voted for. This upholds the key democratic principles of freedom—the ability for an individual to choose who they would like to represent them in parliament, without being pressured or coerced.

Voting is a right, but it can also be seen as a responsibility. Although it's not unlawful to cast an informal (i.e. defective) vote that will not be counted, voting is a civic duty—just like serving on a jury and paying tax. It's up to the individual voter to make informed decisions at election time and vote responsibly.

Australians may also be asked to vote at other times, for instance when changes are proposed to the Australian Constitution. This is the set of rules by which the country can be run; it describes how the federal parliament works and what powers it has. Governments cannot pass laws that conflict with the constitution. To protect our political system, a change to the constitution can only be made if there's a double majority: that is, it must have the support of a majority of Australian voters as well as a majority of voters in at least four states.

1 Voting in elections is not compulsory in Australia.

True False

2 Not everybody was granted the right to vote in Australian elections at the same time.

True False

TARGETING GENERAL CAPABILITIES YEARS 5-6 © PASCAL PRESS ISBN: 9781925726237

Reflecting on intercultural experiences & taking responsibility

3 A secret ballot means that ...

a) nobody else is allowed to know who you are voting for.

b) you are not allowed to know who you are voting for.

c) you are not allowed to know who represents you in parliament.

d) government meetings are held in secret.

4 How does the secret ballot help uphold our democratic principles?

____

____

5 What is the Australian Constitution?

____

6 Most laws are passed by parliament without needing to directly ask voters if they agree with the proposed law—but this is not the case for the Australian Constitution. What is needed for the constitution to be altered?

____

____

7 There is a current movement to formally recognise Indigenous people in the Australian Constitution. How can constitutional rights protect people more than just ordinary laws passed by parliament?

Hint: Think about what changes a future government might be able to make.

____

____

Your view

8 Voting at elections is not compulsory in many democratic countries, including the United States and the United Kingdom. Do you think it should be compulsory in Australia? Why or why not?

____

____

____

____

TARGETING GENERAL CAPABILITIES YEARS 5-6 © PASCAL PRESS ISBN: 9781925726237

HASS – History

Australian Curriculum Links: *ACHASSK107, ACHASSK110, ACHASSK138*

COLONIALISM AND ABORIGINAL PEOPLES

Aboriginal peoples led a very different way of life to that of the Europeans who were to colonise their country, take their land and shatter their way of life. They did not value material possessions or have any industry or military. They had no concept of money and did not practise slavery, and their relationship with the land was not based on owning or exploiting it. To them, the land held, and still holds, a deeply meaningful and spiritual significance.

SETTLERS

The presence of the settlers was accepted by Aboriginal peoples in the early days of the colony, and sometimes even welcomed. This changed as the settlers began to claim more land for farming. Without access to food from their traditional hunting grounds, Aboriginal peoples instead killed the settlers' livestock. This, and other disagreements, caused conflicts between the two groups, leading to a cycle of attacks and retaliations.

WARFARE

These conflicts were fought by the settlers with assistance from the police, as Aboriginal peoples were not considered a significant threat by the British military. Although the Europeans had the upper hand in open country warfare due to their equipment and training, Aboriginal peoples found success when using guerrilla warfare. These stealth and ambush tactics drew on their familiarity with the rugged country. They also waged economic warfare by destroying livestock, property and infrastructure such as telegraph lines. The estimated total number of deaths as a result of these conflicts were around 2500 European settlers and police, and 20,000 Aboriginal peoples.

British settlement brought not only violence to Aboriginal peoples, but also a range of diseases that would decimate their population. The worst of these was the smallpox epidemic of 1789. Aboriginal peoples had no immunity to the disease as they had never been exposed to it before. The Gadigal people of Sydney Cove suffered greatly as a result. By 1791, it was estimated that there were only three Gadigal people remaining.

Source: *Blake's Australian History Guide*, p.34, Pascal Press

Reflecting on intercultural experiences & taking responsibility

Indigenous people shared the same way of life and the same values as the British colonists.

True False

The colonists were initially accepted by the Indigenous Australians.

True False

How did the two groups' relationship with land differ?

___

___

What caused conflict between the colonists and the Indigenous Australians?

a) The colonists continued to claim more land for farming.

b) Indigenous people were denied access to their traditional hunting grounds.

c) Indigenous people killed the colonists' livestock.

d) all of the above

Why do you think the British military did not consider Indigenous people to be a significant threat?

___

___

Circle the correct answer

Indigenous people had to make up for the imbalance of military strength by relying on stealth and ambush tactics, which is a type of *economic / guerrilla warfare*.

Indigenous people had *many / few* citizenship rights during the colonisation era.

Your view

How do you think Indigenous Australians felt when they first had contact with British colonists? What might they have been thinking when people they knew fell ill from smallpox?

___

___

___

___

TARGETING GENERAL CAPABILITIES YEARS 5-6 © PASCAL PRESS ISBN: 9781925726237

Mathematics – Number and Algebra

Australian Curriculum Links: *ACMNA291, ACMNA124*

Timeline – Indigenous Laws passed by the Commonwealth Government

1901 — The Commonwealth of Australia was formed. There was little recognition of Indigenous Australians in the constitution.

1962 — Changes were made to the *Commonwealth Electoral Act 1918*, permitting Indigenous peoples to enrol to vote in federal elections.

1967 — Changes were made to the Australian Constitution, allowing the Commonwealth to pass laws covering Indigenous Australians and for them to be included in the census.

1976 — *Aboriginal Land Rights (Northern Territory) Act 1976* permitted Aboriginal people in the Northern Territory to claim land rights based on traditional occupation.

1989 — *Aboriginal and Torres Strait Islander Commission Act 1989* established ATSIC, a body that delivered and monitored programs and services; it was dismantled in 2005.

1991 — *Council for Aboriginal Reconciliation Act 1991* set up the Council for Aboriginal Reconciliation, later replaced by the current body Reconciliation Australia.

1993 — *Native Title Act 1993* passed following a landmark court case, formally recognising and protecting native title.

1995 — the *Flags Act 1953* was amended so that the Aboriginal and Torres Strait Islander flags were recognised as official Australian flags.

2007 — *Northern Territory National Emergency Response Act 2007*, also known as 'The Intervention'; a set of controversial laws imposing greater controls over the lives of Indigenous people.

2015 — Referendum Council on the constitutional recognition of Indigenous people is established.

Reflecting on intercultural experiences & taking responsibility

INTERCULTURAL UNDERSTANDING

Look at the Commonwealth laws timeline and use your knowledge of mathematics to answer the following questions.

An integer is ...

a) a whole positive number.

b) a whole negative number.

c) a fraction.

d) both a and b.

0 is neither positive nor negative.

True False

0 is not an integer.

True False

Years can be expressed as integers.

True False

Insert dots on the number line to show the approximate position of the 10 years identified in the Timeline.

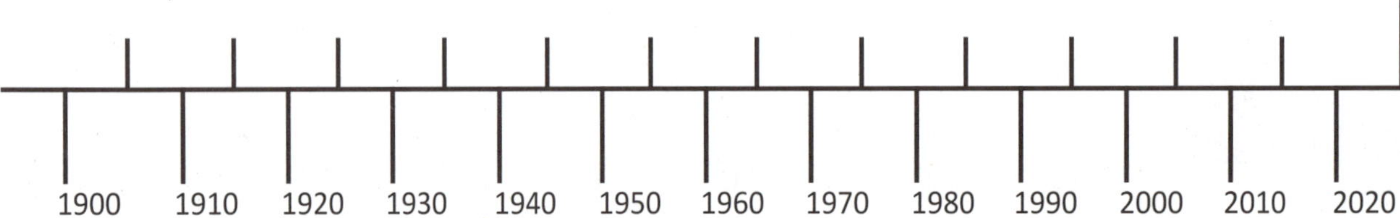

In our number line, the year 1900 is our zero point.

i. Why are there no numbers appearing before 1900?

____

ii. Laws regarding Indigenous people were passed by the colonies before 1900. Would you move in a negative (left) or positive (right) direction from the year 1900 if you wanted to include the relevant years on the number line?

____

How would you describe the pattern of the dots?

Hint: Are they clustered together or spread evenly apart?

____

What does the pattern of the dots tell you about the willingness and ability of the Commonwealth Government to pass laws governing Indigenous Australians?

____

____

The Arts – Visual Arts

Australian Curriculum Link: *ACAVAM114*

The artwork below is part of the Australian Museum's Collection. Titled *Dauma and Garom*, the artwork is made from 'ghost nets', or discarded fishing and trawler nets that litter the oceans. It was created by Indigenous artists from Erub, a remote community in the Torres Strait. The sculptural installation is huge—six metres in size.

"File:Aboriginal Art Ghost net Dauma (30837042055).jpg" by Tony Hisgett from Birmingham, UK is licensed under CC BY 2.0
Source: https://search.creativecommons.org/photos/279b539c-fa07-4b87-90d0-016a2630d7c5

The artwork depicts an Erub story about a crab and a fish who fall in love. But the materials it's made of tell an even deeper story about creation and destruction, and the pressing need to protect the environment. Ghost nets are carried long distances by strong ocean tides. They can float or roll along the sea floor. The nets tangle around reefs and trap fish, crabs and other marine creatures, many of them endangered.

Reflecting on intercultural experiences & taking responsibility

INTERCULTURAL UNDERSTANDING

Examine the image on the previous page and answer the following questions.

1. Who created the artwork? ______________________________

2. What type of artwork is this?

   a) painting b) drawing c) ceramic d) sculpture

3. What does the artwork depict?

   a) a ghost c) a story of the Erub people

   b) a fishing net d) an environmental protest

4. The artwork is based on an Indigenous __________ story.

   a) ghost b) love c) adventure d) creation

5. Do you think the artwork was inspired by observation or imagination or both? Explain your answer.

   ____

   ____

6. What is the artwork made out of?

   ____

7. What message does the choice of material convey?

   ____

   ____

Your turn

8. What litter do you commonly find in your own environment? Brainstorm some ideas about the type of artwork you could produce with that litter, and what message you would be trying to convey.

   ____

   ____

Self-reflection

This unit was about reflecting on intercultural experiences and taking responsibility. What have you learnt about the problems that can arise if people don't try to understand and respect each other's cultures?

____

____

TARGETING GENERAL CAPABILITIES YEARS 5-6 © PASCAL PRESS ISBN: 9781925726237

Recognising culture & developing respect assessment

This unit looked at the reasons why people migrated to Australia and where they came from. Our national identity would be very different if they had not come.

Investigate culture and cultural identity

1. **What do you think Australia would be like today if the White Australia Policy had never been revoked?**

____

____

2. **What are some of the things we would have missed out on if the waves of immigration had never happened?**

____

____

Explore and compare cultural knowledge, beliefs and practices

Different cultures have unique ways of celebrating important events, such as weddings. Do some research into the wedding traditions of a culture that you do NOT belong to and answer the following questions.

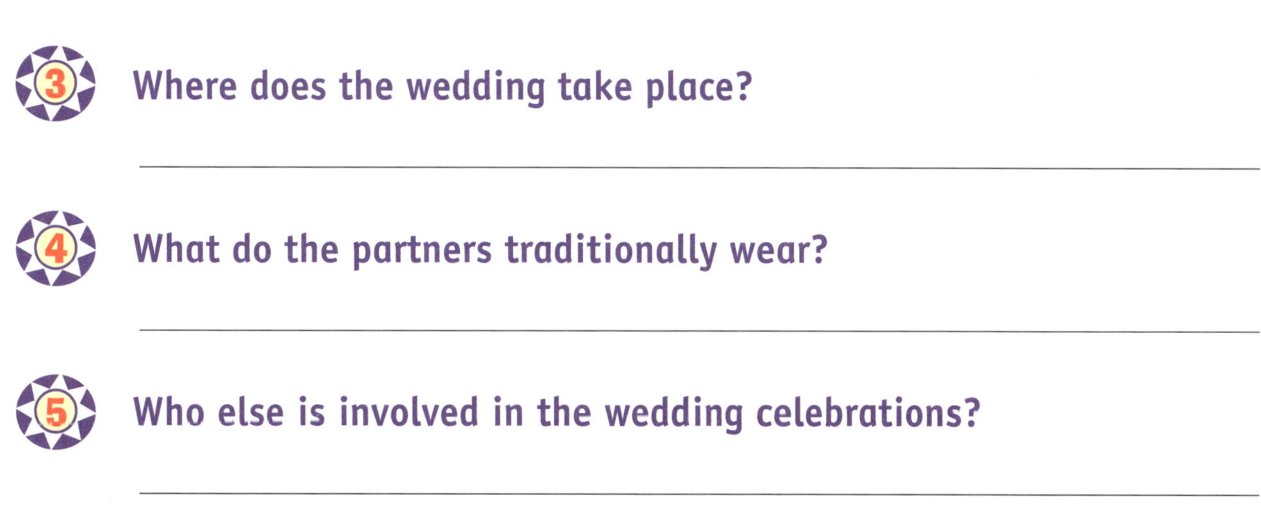

3. **Where does the wedding take place?**

____

4. **What do the partners traditionally wear?**

____

5. **Who else is involved in the wedding celebrations?**

____

____

6 How long do the celebrations typically last?

____

7 Is a special type of food served to guests?

____

____

8 List some of the important traditions that mark the event (e.g. in Western weddings the bride throws the flower bouquet).

____

____

____

Develop respect for cultural diversity

Cultural diversity offers many opportunities within our society. Use words from the word bank to complete the sentences below.

Word bank

understand skills ways enjoy

9 Workers from different backgrounds bring new __________ into the country.

10 Migrants bring their cuisines with them, which we can all share and ________.

11 A diverse society means that we can _________ the world better.

12 People from different backgrounds have different ________ of solving existing problems.

TARGETING GENERAL CAPABILITIES YEARS 5-6 © PASCAL PRESS ISBN: 9781925726237

Interacting & empathising with others assessment

This unit looked at the issue of climbing Uluru and how the traditional owners felt when visitors ignored their wishes and entered a sacred space. It looked at ways that compromises were made to satisfy the desire of tourists to explore the area while at the same time respecting the wishes of the traditional owners.

Communicate across cultures

The famous landmark has two names: Uluru and Ayers Rock. Uluru is its Indigenous name and it comes from the Pitjantjatjara language. In 1873, an explorer became the first non-Aboriginal person to see the site. He named it Ayers Rock after Sir Henry Ayer, the Chief Secretary of South Australia. The name was officially changed to Ayers Rock/Uluru in 1993, and then the order of the names was reversed to Uluru/Ayers Rock in 2002. This is still its official name, although people refer to the site by either name.

1 Which name do you prefer to use and why? Do you think it matters which name you choose? Explain your answer.

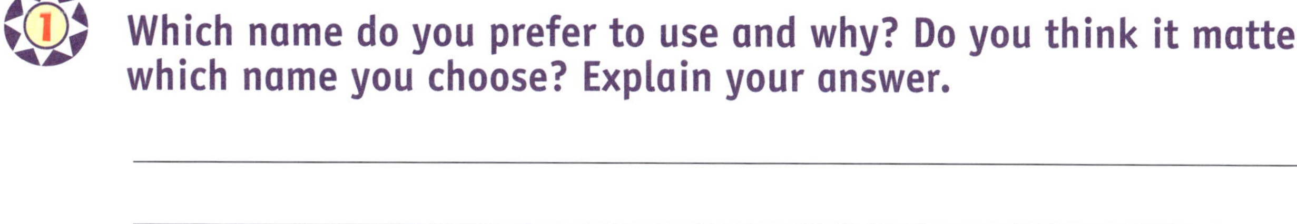

Consider and develop multiple perspectives

Different groups of people have different views and perspectives when it comes to visiting sites of Indigenous cultural significance. Draw lines to match the issue with the group of people that you would most expect it to belong to.

Issue	Group of people
i. whether tours are profitable	a. environmental activists
ii. the need to protect the site's ecology	b. tourists
iii. the availability of jobs in the area	c. tour companies
iv. the site's sacred significance	d. local workers
v. the ability to visit and enjoy the site	e. traditional owners

3. Which issue do you personally think is the most important? Explain your answer.

4. Do you think it is possible for solutions to be reached that satisfy everybody—or at least most people? What should people do to try to reach such a solution?

Empathise with others

5. Assume you are a member of the Anangu people. One day you discover that a group of tourists breached the ban and climbed Uluru. Write a diary entry to describe how you feel.

TARGETING GENERAL CAPABILITIES YEARS 5-6 © PASCAL PRESS ISBN: 9781925726237

Reflecting on intercultural experiences & taking responsibility assessment

This unit is about how the legal system recognises and treats Indigenous Australians, and how this has changed since Federation. Many advances have been made, but there is still work to be done to build respect and trust between the wider community and Indigenous Australians.

Reflect on intercultural experiences

There is increasing recognition of the atrocities committed against Indigenous Australians. Some were performed in an attempt to oppress them, while others were the result of misguided attempts to help them. What have you learnt about the need to understand a culture before trying to pass laws that affect them?

____

____

____

Challenge stereotypes and prejudices

Often people are judged on what they look like. These are things which people can't control, and they don't tell us anything about what they are really like. This is both unfair and wrong. In order to understand someone, we have to stop generalising and look beyond appearances.

Find words in the word bank that only show what people look like on the outside (external factors) and those that show what they are really like on the inside (internal factors). Fill in the table.

Word bank

friendly smart colouring race brave gender

weight sporty talented height age caring

External factors	Internal factors

What are some of the dangers of judging people purely because they belong to a particular group or culture? Consider the problems faced by the people being judged, as well as the effect on society as a whole.

Mediate cultural difference

Reconciliation Australia is an independent organisation that works to build trust and respect between Indigenous Australians and the non-indigenous population. Its vision is based on five dimensions or elements that work together, as listed below.

Visit their website at https://www.reconciliation.org.au/ and in your own words write what is meant by each element.

i. race relations

ii. equality and equity

iii. unity

iv. institutional integrity

v. historical acceptance

TARGETING GENERAL CAPABILITIES YEARS 5-6 © PASCAL PRESS ISBN: 9781925726237

PERSONAL & SOCIAL CAPABILITY

Unit 1

English – Language 1 A fad is something that a group of people gets very excited about for a short period of time. 2 d 3 A fact is objective and can be proven to be true or false, while an opinion is subjective and is based on someone's thoughts or feelings. The statement is an opinion. 4 c 5 true 6 false 7 i. Objective – it's appropriate because it's a history article not an opinion piece. ii. Subjective – it's appropriate because it's a casual and private family setting. 8 Personal responses will vary.

Mathematics – Statistics and Probability 1 c 2 a 3 b 4 i. dabbing ii. ice bucket challenge 5 30/30 or 100% 6 12/30 or 40% 7 They were incorrect because 30 children said they'd dabbed and there were 30 in the class. They probably didn't consider dabbing to be a fad, even though it is. 8 Personal responses will vary.

HASS – Economics and Business 1 Needs are things required for survival or to maintain a basic standard of living, while wants aren't essential, but they are desirable. 2 Fads are usually wants, they're not essential because they keep changing.

3

Needs	Wants
water	chocolate bar
everyday clothes	roller shoes
staple foods	computer game
shoes	party dress
housing	soft drink

4 d 5 true 6 true 7 Trade-offs need to be made because wants are unlimited while resources are limited, and so people have to make a choice as to what they want the most. 8 Personal responses will vary.

Health & Physical Education 1 People can lose their balance and fall, which can cause injury. 2 The water container can fall on the person's head and hurt them, or they might catch a bad cold. 3 Cinnamon powder is very fine and caustic, it can get in people's lungs and cause damage. 4 false 5 false 6 true 7 d; 8 Personal responses will vary.

Unit 2

English – Language 1 a 2 b 3 d 4 to provide step-by-step instructions on how to build a scarecrow 5 No, the instructions are too vague and hard to visualise.

6

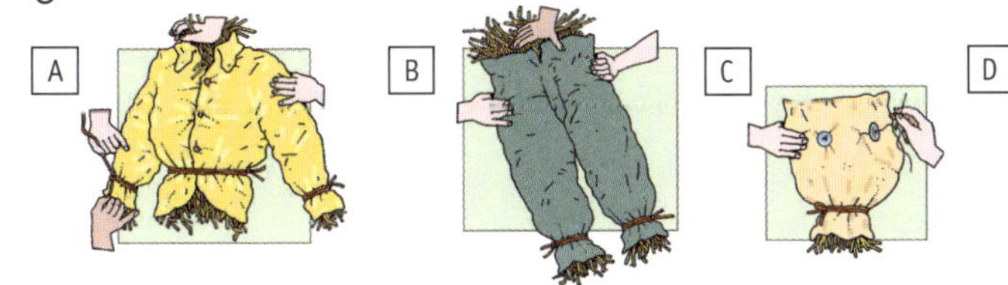

7 true 8 Personal responses will vary.

ANSWERS

HASS – Geography 1 c 2 Schools are near residential areas so that children and families will have easy access and not have to travel too far. 3 i. the landscape features of the area ii. the needs of the people who live there 4 crowded, high-density living, many busy roads, not much green space 5 It's unlikely Faruq has much or any garden at home. This may be his only opportunity to do some gardening, which he enjoys. 6 true 7 d 8 Personal responses will vary.

Science 1 So that any differences in the results are not the result of pre-existing differences 2 a 3 b 4 c 5 Pot 1 because it had everything the plant needed to survive 6 Pot 2 would have grown nearly as well because it would sometimes get watered by rainfall. Pots 3 and 4 might not have survived at all because they each missed an important factor. If they did survive, they wouldn't have thrived. 7 You need to spend time caring for the plants and working out what they need to thrive. 8 Personal responses will vary.

Technologies – Design and Technologies 1 It reduces the need for long-distance transport and storage, so there'd be fewer carbon emissions and pollution and less expense. 2 i. climatic – rainfall, sunlight, humidity, frost, etc. ii. soil – sandy, clay, fertile, barren etc. 3 d 4 c 5 false 6 Toilet wastewater can contain disease-carrying germs and contaminate the soil and the plants. 7 & 8 Personal responses will vary.

Health & Physical Education 1 grain foods, vegetables and legumes/beans 2 c 3 alcohol, soft drinks, chips, processed meats, sweets 4 fruit, vegetables and legumes/beans 5 i. exercise ii. social contact and community involvement 6 false 7 true 8 Personal responses will vary.

Unit 3

English – Literature 1 c 2 a 3 To highlight some of the problems of climate change and to gather support for a climate strike 4 i. the first stanza ii. the second stanza 5 intense, madness, emergency, insist, kick up a storm 6 d 7 To create a sense of urgency, also the words are mostly commands 8 Personal responses will vary.

HASS – Civics and Citizenship 1 To raise public awareness of climate change and to make demands that the government take urgent action to reduce carbon emissions and increase renewable energy 2 false 3 true 4 d 5 b 6 i. Kowalski thought the strikes were a waste of time and protestors should go to uni to learn how to save the planet. ii. Smythe was concerned about children suffering from climate anxiety. iii. Voyle doesn't believe climate change is real. 7 A combination of both because the effects are global, but each nation has a responsibility to take action. 8 Personal responses will vary.

Science 1 b 2 i. We orbit at the right distance from the sun (within the Goldilocks zone). ii. Our atmosphere acts like a greenhouse, trapping in heat. 3 Too much heat would escape from the Earth, likely making it too cold for human habitation (like on Mars). 4 false 5 true 6 d 7 i. Personal responses will vary. ii. Some people think climate change is natural and not caused by humans, some might not want to change their habits, some might fear the disruption that comes from moving away from fossil fuels, some might worry they'll suffer economic loss or lose their jobs, etc. 8 Personal responses will vary.

TARGETING GENERAL CAPABILITIES YEARS 5-6 © PASCAL PRESS ISBN: 9781925726237

Mathematics – Statistics and Probability 1 b 2 a 3 d 4 $\frac{1}{4}$ 5 0.25 6 25% 7 d 8 Tomorrow's forecast is more likely to be accurate because many factors can change over time, and these changes affect the possible outcomes – e.g. winds might move faster than predicted and/or change direction. This is why forecasts are generally updated at least daily.

Health & Physical Education 1 negative 2 positive 3 d 4 false 5 true 6 Helpful, because he didn't deny their concerns, rather he made a constructive suggestion for a solution. 7 Unhelpful, because he refused to accept their concerns and accused them of attention-seeking behaviour. 8 Personal responses will vary.

Unit 4

English – Language 1 d 2 c 3 c 4 informal – regular use of contractions e.g. 'we're', 'I'll', also in first person speaking directly to the reader 5 b 6 Objective language states the plain facts without emotion, while subjective language shows the writer's emotions, opinions and point of view. 7 i. objective ii. subjective 8 Personal responses will vary.

HASS – History 1 false 2 true 3 c 4 How did you feel? How long did it take to recover? Did you have any lasting damage? Did it affect your work, your family, etc.? How long did it take for life to go back to normal? Did you struggle financially? 5 primary 6 It struck young, otherwise healthy people, it was severe, it was very contagious. The makeshift nature of the crowded hospital shows they weren't really prepared for the scale of the problem. 7 state borders closed, self-isolation, quarantine, cancelled events, closed businesses, face masks, hand hygiene 8 Personal responses will vary.

HASS – Economics and Business 1 c 2 d 3 The economy can shrink due to the decreased demand for goods and services. 4 toilet paper, paper towels, hand sanitisers, face masks, flour, pasta, canned and frozen food, etc. 5 Panic buying can lead to genuine shortages as producers and retailers can't keep up with demand, and vulnerable people may miss out on what they need. Some people bought out too much and re-sold items at exorbitant prices. Fights broke out as people competed for goods. 6 true 7 false 8 Personal responses will vary.

Technologies – Design and Technologies 1 People who became seriously ill needed the life-saving equipment. 2 It is hard, especially in the early days of the outbreak, because they do not know how many people will get sick, and of those how many will require medical equipment. 3 false 4 true 5 true 6 d 7 The equipment will most likely be available sooner as the hospitals won't have to wait for international shipping, which tends to be interrupted and delayed during a pandemic. Also, local equipment might be more suited to Australian conditions and be able to be used with existing systems. 8 Personal responses will vary.

Technologies – Digital Technologies 1 true 2 false 3 false 4 d 5 They could arrange to all go into the documents at the same time each day. 6 No writing negative, sarcastic or rude comments on each other's diaries, no deleting other people's entries, no bullying. 7 No sharing of material, images, secrets etc. outside of the Google Docs diary environment. 8 Personal responses will vary.

ANSWERS

ANSWERS

PERSONAL & SOCIAL CAPABILITY ASSESSMENTS

Answers are not provided for tasks where personal responses will vary.

Self-awareness

5

Seeing learners	*Hearing learners*	*Writing learners*	*Doing learners*
Look at diagrams	Listen to teacher	Read book	Follow demonstration
Look at infographics	Listen to podcast	Write notes	Perform experiment

Self-management

4

Short-term goals	Medium-term goals	Long-term goals
finish homework	pass end-of-term exams	become a doctor
practise piano	learn a new instrument	live near the beach
go to friend's house	learn another language	travel the world

6 Faruq took the initiative because he saw that there was a problem and he wanted to solve it. He worked independently by searching for solutions online and then by trying to make the scarecrow himself. He kept going, using trial and error, until he succeeded. He reached his goal of making a scarecrow to protect the school's kitchen garden.

7 Keep trying, be positive, ask for help, learn more, take a chance, enjoy the process.

Social awareness

1

Who?	Concerned about climate change	Support climate strikes
Dylan Miller	yes	yes
Ming Chan	yes	yes
John Kowalski	yes	no
Camilla Smythe	yes	no
Robin Voyle	no	no

2 They might feel the problem is urgent and they need to raise public awareness quickly. They may feel this is the only way they have to address the problem.

3 They might feel that the problem isn't real, or that better action can be taken, or that the strikes cause too much disruption and anxiety.

4 Responses will vary, but may include: i. hindered – overly negative, pessimistic and emotionally charged ii helped – rational, determined and optimistic iii helped – rational and offered alternative solution iv helped – expressed concern for those involved v hindered – hostile, close-minded and suspicious.

TARGETING GENERAL CAPABILITIES YEARS 5-6 © PASCAL PRESS ISBN: 9781925726237

6

Positive effect	Negative effect
discussing	ignoring
listening	sarcasm
patience	interrupting
taking turns	shouting
applauding	booing

Social management

2 The government would have considered how effective masks are, how easy it is to obtain a mask, how affordable they are, how easy it is to catch COVID-19 both with and without a mask, how deadly it is, and what the hospital's capacity currently was for treating people.

3 There were competing considerations, including weighing up the potential benefits of mask-wearing with: the restriction on people's individual liberties, how unpopular the laws might be with the public, the difficulty and expense of enforcing the law, the cost and potential difficulty in obtaining masks, the fact that some people might have medical reasons for not wearing masks.

4 i. explain ii. talk iii. listen iv. respect v. most

INTERCULTURAL UNDERSTANDING

Unit 5

English – Literacy 1 b 2 The purpose is to explain the various reasons people migrated to Australia in the twentieth century, showing the difference between push and pull factors. 3 a 4 The structure makes the material easy to follow because the headings help the reader locate the relevant information. Each paragraph contains a single idea, and the division of the text into the two halves of push and pull factors makes the difference between the notions clear. 5 b 6 The poster is bright and colourful, featuring happy people raising their hands in greeting in a prosperous-looking rural setting. It is trying to portray Australia as a friendly, welcoming, energetic and wealthy land. 7 This has no pictures apart from the Southern Cross. It has much more print text, and it is coloured red, white and blue. This one is aimed at British people who are obviously fluent in the language. It also plays on a sense of patriotism. The first poster may be aimed at Europeans who were needed to come and work in Australia but may not have been so fluent in English or motivated by a sense of British patriotism. 8 Personal responses will vary.

HASS – History 1 Push factors push people out of a country while pull factors pull people towards a country. 2 d 3 d 4 It was a young and growing country and needed skilled people to join the workforce and make the economy bigger. Also, a sparsely populated country might have been more vulnerable to attack post WWII. 5 primary 6 Greece 7 He had skills that enabled him to get a good job and he already had family living here. 8 Personal responses will vary.

HASS – Geography 1 North West Europe 2 decreased 3 i. Other Americas (Central America, Caribbean and Americas) ii. North Africa 4 d 5 true 6 false 7 There are more likely to be existing migrant populations there, more work opportunities and generally a milder climate along the coast. 8 Personal responses will vary.

The Arts – Dance 1 true 2 true 3 space, time, dynamics, relationship 4 The dancers are up high—they are standing upright, legs and arms raised. This indicates a joyful, energetic, uplifting experience. 5 The dance looks as if it would be fast. They look like they're leaping; their feet are blurred by movement in the photograph, and their costumes are flapping. 6 The dancers are touching and closely connected. They are performing the same movements and facing in the same direction, showing a strong sense of communal identity and fellowship. 7 Answers may include: music, food, sport, celebrations, clothing and costumes, games and toys, etc. 8 Personal responses will vary.

Health & Physical Education 1 To coincide with the United Nations' International Day for the Elimination of Racial Discrimination. It's the Australian response to the international initiative. 2 Everyone Belongs 3 It shows people of different shapes, sizes and colours wearing different costumes all standing together and holding hands. 4 d 5 Orange is bright, cheerful and optimistic. There aren't many orange national flags, so it doesn't feel that any one nation is being favoured. 6 People can feel alienated and unwelcome, divisions can arise in society, there may be discrimination, prejudice and disharmony. 7 There'll be a greater sense of community cohesion, access to a greater range of cultural items and events, an opportunity to explore and enjoy new ideas and new employment opportunities; 8 Personal responses will vary.

Unit 6

English – Language 1 a 2 They acknowledge that their correct way of saying the group name is hard for others to pronounce, and Anangu means 'The People'. 3 b 4 b 5 To ensure his message is clear to everyone, to show respect for his audience by being formal and polite, to make his point strongly while staying rational and calm. 6 true 7 true 8 Personal responses will vary.

HASS – Civics and Citizenship 1 a 2 false 3 true 4 d 5 lobby 6 committee 7 law 8 Personal responses will vary.

HASS – Geography 1 Sustainability refers to living in a way that meets the needs of the present without harming those of future generations. 2 They realised some seasons were better for hunting/fishing, others for gathering. Some moved according to the seasons, ensuring the food sources had time to regenerate. 3 true 4 false 5 The knock-on effect is when something happens that causes other things to happen. In this case, if the supply of

a plant or animal runs out, it affects other living things that rely on it. 6 Regularly burning small patches over large areas creates a pasture-like landscape. 7 It limited the intensity of bushfires, attracted animals to the regrowth and made it easier to move and hunt. 8 Personal responses will vary.

Science 1 d 2 The Bureau of Meteorology, ATSIC, and Monash University's Centre for Indigenous Studies, to share traditional Indigenous knowledge about climate and seasons 3 false 4 true 5 true 6 Indigenous – There are more seasons and they are shorter, making them more likely to be precise. Also, they were developed based on observations of local conditions, rather than being imported from conditions observed overseas. 7 c 8 Personal responses will vary.

Technologies – Design and Technologies 1 true 2 d 3 competing considerations between tour operators and the Anangu people 4 They want people to see their culture, which will help them to understand and respect it. 5 Involve indigenous people in the planning so that they benefit financially as well as having their culture protected and respected, while tourists enjoy an authentic cultural experience. 6 It probably took so long because tourist companies didn't want to lose money, and because some tourists wanted to be free to climb. 7 The Mala and Liru walks, which are guided by the Anangu and other rangers 8 Personal responses will vary.

ANSWERS

Unit 7

English – Literacy 1 1901 2 i. two ii. zero 3 c 4 They were meant to protect Aboriginal people, but they actually controlled their lives in many intrusive ways e.g. needing permission to marry, who they could work for, and how much they were paid. 5 c 6 Information about two referenda to be held, including the one regarding the recognition of Aboriginals. It includes arguments for and against the proposed alterations, and it shows what the proposed alterations were. 7 The State Library of South Australia, either in person or online 8 Responses will vary but may include: What did the reforms actually change in the constitution? Were laws created that reflected the reforms? Did Indigenous Australians benefit from the reforms? How did they benefit? Did the reforms go far enough? What more needs to be done? etc.

HASS – Civics and Citizenship 1 false 2 true 3 a 4 By voting in secret, we can select the person or party we'd like to represent us in parliament without feeling pressured to vote for somebody we don't want to vote for. 5 The set of rules by which the country can be run 6 A double majority, i.e. a majority of voters in a majority of states 7 Ordinary laws can be changed without parliament asking voters to agree, so a government could remove people's rights in the future. If enshrined in the constitution, a future government could not take away those rights without a referendum. 8 Personal responses will vary.

HASS – History 1 false 2 true 3 The Indigenous people's relationship with land was spiritual, while the colonists saw land as something to be owned and exploited. 4 d 5 They were relatively low in numbers and didn't have the same equipment, training and military strength as the colonists. 6 guerrilla 7 few 8 Personal responses will vary.

Mathematics – Number and Algebra 1 d 2 true 3 false 4 true

5

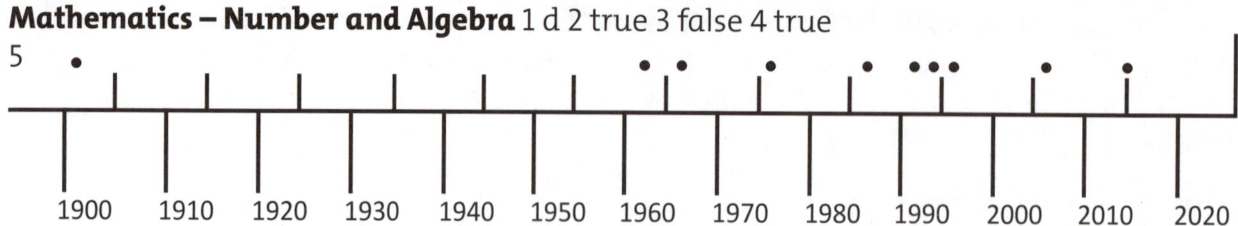

6 i. the Commonwealth was founded in 1901, so it could not pass laws before it existed ii. negative iii. 1890 – It would appear to the left of 1900. 7 clustered together towards the right-hand side 8 The Commonwealth was constitutionally unable to do much before the 1967 amendments. More laws were passed as time went by, reflecting society's increasing recognition of the need to recognise and protect Indigenous rights.

The Arts – Visual Arts 1 Indigenous artists from the Erub community in the Torres Strait 2 d 3 c 4 b 5 Both – It depicts part of a story (imagination) and is an identifiable likeness of a crab (observation). 6 discarded fishing and trawling nets 7 The need to protect the environment from ocean litter—it takes dangerous material and uses it to create rather than destroy. 8 Personal responses will vary.

ANSWERS

INTERCULTURAL UNDERSTANDING ASSESSMENTS

Answers are not provided for tasks where personal responses will vary.

Recognising culture & developing respect

1 Australia would be more homogenous because the Australian-born citizens and British migrants would share the same cultural background. The population would be much smaller—perhaps too small for the economy to grow, so it might be a much poorer country.

2 Ethnic-food and fusion-food restaurants, milk bars, household items such as woks, sports, games, clothing fashions, skilled workers in various fields (e.g. medicine, manufacturing, engineering), décor, music and artwork, etc.

9 skills 10 enjoy 11 understand 12 ways

Interacting & empathising with others

2 i. c ii. a iii. d iv. e v. b

4 It might not be possible to find a solution that suits absolutely everyone, but it should be possible to find one that suits most people. It would require open and honest communication, an attempt to understand other peoples' perspectives and a willingness to compromise.

TARGETING GENERAL CAPABILITIES YEARS 5-6 © PASCAL PRESS ISBN: 9781925726237

Reflecting on intercultural experiences & taking responsibility

2

External factors	Internal factors
colouring	friendly
race	smart
gender	brave
weight	sporty
height	talented
age	caring

3 It can lead to unfair treatment and discrimination, and people can be disadvantaged in many areas including education, jobs, housing, access to services, income, healthcare, etc. It can also lead to resentment and tensions within society.

4 i. All Australians should understand and value all cultures, building non-racist relationships based on trust.

ii. Indigenous people should be able to participate equally in opportunities that other Australians have.

iii. Australian society should recognise indigenous culture and heritage as part of our shared identity.

iv. Institutions including business, community groups and politicians should support reconciliation.

v. Everyone should accept past mistakes, make amends and ensure the wrongs aren't repeated.

Targeting General Capabilities
PERSONAL & SOCIAL CAPABILITY
INTERCULTURAL UNDERSTANDING

Years 5 & 6

ISBN: 9781925726237

Published by Pascal Press
PO Box 250
Glebe NSW 2037
www.pascalpress.com.au
contact@pascalpress.com.au

Author: Stella Tarakson
Publisher: Lynn Dickinson
Editor: Marie Theodore
Typesetter/Designer: Stacey Grainger
Illustrator: Paul Lennon

Printed in South Korea by Prinpia Co., Ltd.